One

One Line Drive

A LIFE-THREATENING INJURY
AND A FAITH-FUELED COMEBACK

DANIEL PONCE DE LEON

WITH TOM ZENNER

Faith
Words
New York • Nashville

FaithWords
Hachette Book Group
1290 Avenue of the Americas, New York, NY 10104
faithwords.com
twitter.com/faithwords

First Edition: March 2021

FaithWords is a division of Hachette Book Group, Inc. The FaithWords name and logo are trademarks of Hachette Book Group, Inc.

The publisher is not responsible for websites (or their content) that are not owned by the publisher.

The Hachette Speakers Bureau provides a wide range of authors for speaking events. To find out more, go to www.hachettespeakersbureau.com or call (866) 376-6591.

Library of Congress Cataloging-in-Publication Data

Names: Ponce de Leon, Daniel, 1992- author. | Zenner, Tom, author.
Title: One line drive : a life-threatening injury and a faith-fueled comeback / Daniel Ponce de Leon and Tom Zenner.
Description: Nashville : FaithWords, 2021.
Identifiers: LCCN 2020042922 | ISBN 9781546034551 (Hardcover) | ISBN 9781546034575 (eBook)
Subjects: LCSH: Ponce de Leon, Daniel, 1992- | Pitchers (Baseball)—California—Biography. | Baseball players—United States—Biography. | Baseball players—Religious life—United States. | St. Louis Cardinals (Baseball team)—History. | Major League Baseball (Organization)—History.
Classification: LCC GV865.P666 A3 2021 | DDC 796.357092 [B]—dc23
LC record available at https://lccn.loc.gov/2020042922

ISBNs: 978-1-5460-3455-1(hardcover); 978-1-5460-4173-3 (special signed edition); 978-1-5460-4174-0 (signed edition); 978-1-5460-3457-5 (ebook)

Printed in the United States of America

LSC_C

Printing 1, 2021

To my loving wife and family who have supported me in becoming the best person, husband, and father that I can be. I love you.

CONTENTS

CHAPTER 1

A MIRACLE DISGUISED
AS A NIGHTMARE

I did not know the street address of Principal Park in Des Moines, Iowa, home of the Iowa Cubs, the day I first stepped onto its field. Why would I? I had never been in that stadium. I didn't even know the address of my home stadium back in Tennessee. At the time I was a pitcher for the Memphis Redbirds, the Triple-A minor league affiliate of the St. Louis Cardinals. Since I had started the 2017 season off pretty well, I was hoping my days in any minor league ballpark would be numbered. There were no guarantees about when it would happen, but I knew if I continued to pitch well, with the grace of God, there would be a chance I'd be called up at some point to pitch in a

Major League Baseball game. I learned the address of that stadium in Des Moines much later, and once I heard it, I knew I would never forget it: *1 Line Drive.*

Just like the play that almost killed me.

It was May 9, 2017, in the top of the second inning of the fourth game of our series with the Cubs, and I was pitching for the Redbirds. The time was a little past one thirty on a beautiful spring afternoon, when, in an instant, my life changed forever. At the time, I had no idea that almost dying that day would be a gift from God.

Everybody remembers random details from important days in their life. Thinking back to certain milestones like special birthdays, the days on which your children were born, your wedding day, or some big achievement or recognition at work, most people have certain parts of those days lodged in their memory bank. What I remember most vividly about that day is that the bottom of my baseball spikes were green.

The Cubs expected a big crowd that day, and in order to make the field appear more vibrant, the groundskeepers had painted portions of the grass green. At some point, I walked right through it, and when I looked at the bottom of my shoes when I was on the mound, they were covered with fresh green paint.

It was an afternoon game, rare for a weekday, but there was a special promotion the Iowa Cubs were doing for schoolkids around the city, so the game started at one o'clock. Having a chance to go to a baseball game instead of school? I don't know many kids who wouldn't sign up for that. I wish that had been an option when I was growing up. There's a restaurant in Des Moines called Mullets, which is well known and close to the hotel where we were staying, and I was planning on having breakfast there before heading to the ballpark to get ready to make my start. The place was popular, and on this day packed, so I went to Plan B and ended up having a lighter meal than I normally would on a day I was pitching. It would be the only food I ate the entire day.

My inspiration on days I am pitching comes from Christian music. It's as much a part of my routine as listening to the national anthem. It's something that takes my mind and my spirit where they need to be to compete. I have playlists on my phone, and during warm-ups that morning I had those familiar worship tunes in my ear as I got ready. It was still very early in the season, but I was off to a good start, and I was hoping to continue to pitch well against Iowa. The Cardinals had promoted me at the beginning of the season from Double-A to Triple-A, so I was now just one step away from the big leagues.

If a pitcher on the major league roster got hurt, I could get a call to replace him, so every game was ultra-important, as I hoped to constantly be on the radar screen of the decision makers in St. Louis. In my first game of the season, I had struck out eight batters in four innings, and I believed if I kept pitching like I had so far in 2017, I'd be with the Cardinals soon.

Back in Florida, my girlfriend, Jenn, was at home with our young son, Casen. As a starting pitcher, I played only about every five days, so it was easy for Jenn and her family in Florida, and my dad and other family members of mine in California, to follow my career by watching games online on days that I started. They could tune in to my one game per week and stay caught up. Jenn had been visiting frequently since we'd left Florida in late March, and she already had a plane ticket booked for her and Casen to come to Memphis on Friday. I was excited to see them in a few days and fired up to pitch on this sunny and beautiful day.

The first inning took me longer to settle in than I wanted. I gave up a couple of hits, but no runs, and I walked out to the mound to start the second inning, making note of the backdrop in the outfield. In most ballparks there is what's called "a batter's eye" in center field. It's a black or dark wall that is there to provide a backdrop for hitters so that they can pick up the white baseball being pitched to them. In Iowa they don't have that. They just have openness in the outfield, and then far off in the distance you can see the gold tower on top of the Iowa State Capitol Building, with the sunlight bouncing off it. This makes daytime games there tough on the hitters to recognize pitch spin and tracking. That means pitchers generally have an advantage, although I hadn't yet shown that.

The leadoff hitter for the Cubs to start the second inning was Victor Caratini, a left-hander I was facing for the first time. My catcher gave me a sign to throw a two-seam fastball. I agreed with the choice and gave him a quick nod. My fastball was a pitch that had been working fairly well since the season started. I went into my windup to deliver the first pitch of the inning.

As soon as the ball left my hand, I wished I could have reached out and taken it back. I knew I hadn't located it where I intended to. In moments like that, you hope the batter either fouls it off or keeps his bat on his shoulder. I knew it was a mistake. The ball started on its proper course down the middle of the plate, but instead of sinking down and away from a left-handed hitter, like it was supposed to, this pitch didn't alter its course. It hung right in the middle, exactly the type of pitching mistake that experienced professional hitters jump on.

There are two more things I remember about that pitch,

which was my final pitch of the 2017 season. Two sounds, very similar, and spaced maybe a second apart from each other at the most. The first sound was Caratini's bat hitting the ball… immediately followed by the sound of the ball hitting my head.

People ask me frequently if I saw the ball coming or if I remember it hitting me directly above my right eye. Believe it or not, I do remember being hit. I can remember seeing the seams on the ball spinning as it flew right back to where it came from. I instinctively raised my arms to try to deflect the ball, but there simply wasn't enough time. I got my glove and arm up in a self-defense motion, but it did not block the ball or even slow it down one bit. I was able to turn my head to the side at the very last instant, or it would have been a direct hit to my face. I fell to the ground. Usually when a ball strikes an object at a speed of almost 100 miles per hour, it will deflect to the right or left and roll away. When the ball made contact with my temple, it flew directly into the air a few feet, and then came straight down, planting into the ground just in front of the pitcher's mound. My head had essentially absorbed the full force of the impact.

At this time in my career I wore glasses when I pitched, and the glasses I had on that day somehow did not break. They didn't even crack. Something else many people find surprising is that the force of the ball hitting my head did not open a gaping wound and cause external bleeding. It turned out that there was excessive bleeding taking place on the *inside* of my skull near my brain, but as horrific as the whole scene looked and sounded, I seemed to be okay, from the outside anyway. In those early moments, I didn't think it was a serious injury. Maybe at worst, I figured, I had suffered a concussion. I had played football all the way through high school, and I'd had my bell rung on numerous occasions, but I was always able to continue to play. It had never stopped me before. In those moments lying there, I was thinking that I'd probably have to rest, take a concussion protocol test, and be back on the field within a few days.

Later, I learned that while I was lying on the ground, trying to convince myself I wasn't seriously injured, the ballpark had taken on an eerie stillness. The eight thousand people in the stands had instantly gone quiet. The broadcast video shows Caratini visibly stunned as he stood at first base, and both he and the Cubs first-base coach had their hands on their heads in a show of helplessness and concern. My catcher, Alberto Rosario, sprinted to the mound to check on me, fearing the worst. He turned to wave for trainer Scott Ensell to join him on the mound, but Scott was already halfway there, handling the situation as professionally and flawlessly as humanly possible. He had no idea it would be more than two and a half weeks before he would leave the state of Iowa.

Scott would later tell me that I got one part of the incident wrong. I had believed I'd never lost consciousness, but he explained that when he arrived at the mound, for at least the first few seconds, I was unconscious. "I saw the play, and at first I thought the ball caught you near your shoulder area or near the top of your body," Scott said. "But the way you dropped, I knew it was your head. When I first got to you, I said, 'Ponce, where did that get you?' You didn't say anything and I knew you were out."

Scott asked me a couple of other questions, and when I didn't respond, he made a motion to the Cubs trainer to execute the emergency protocol for the stadium. Scott kept talking to me, asking me questions about where I'd been hit, and finally I responded. He said I was real quiet, and kind of muffled, but I said, "head."

My teammates rushed to the dugout railing, leaping over it and spilling onto the field, hoping to do something to help. It's a terrible feeling when someone is injured, and I know from my experience the only thing a teammate can do in a moment like that is to say a prayer and ask God to be with the injured player.

I don't remember a lot about the moments that followed.

I've had to rely on the memories of others who were there and the footage from that day to piece it all together. But I remember that the crowd was deadly silent as Scott continued to evaluate the best course of action. I remember Scott grilling me, trying to make a determination of how much I knew.

"I'm going to ask you some questions, Ponce," he told me. "Hang with me. What is your name? Where did you get hit?" I heard the question clearly and answered him correctly. "When is your birthday?" Scott followed up.

The video replays that ran countless times on ESPN and local newscasts around the country showed the situation was dire. And it might be hard to believe, but while I was lying on the ground motionless, with my shocked and concerned teammates lined up around me, I was not only answering Scott's questions correctly, but I was able to ask our trainer a question of my own. "Can I get up and go to the clubhouse?" I pleaded.

"No," Scott told me emphatically. He kept asking me the same types of basic questions, while getting word to the emergency staff on duty at the ballpark to immediately call 911.

I thank God Scott was there, trained to handle situations like mine, because I was still trying to convince myself things weren't serious. Maybe it's a stinger, I thought, a common ailment that I had experienced as a football player.

As the stretcher was carried to the mound, my instincts and pride were still telling me to stand up and walk away from this whole scene. I remember thinking how embarrassing it all was, with the concerned crowd of people standing around me. But even as I was trying to say no to the stretcher, I was starting to experience some changes in the way I was feeling. Just like that, the pain was really setting in.

Scott continued to evaluate what he was dealing with and how bad things actually were. He was as thorough and cautious as he could be, trusting his years of training and following every conceivable procedure and protocol by the book. When I think about those moments now, I know that Scott literally held my life in his hands. One delay or wrong decision by him would have changed the outcome.

He placed his hands underneath me as he stabilized my head so it wouldn't move. "My neck is not broken," I told him. I pleaded with him one last time, "Can I just get up and go to the clubhouse?"

The stretcher arrived and was placed next to me. The medics secured my head as they got ready for the delicate transfer needed to take me off the field. "I'm fine, Scott," I said.

"If you're fine," he said, "then just go ahead and give a

thumbs-up to the fans so they can see it on TV too." I did what he asked, delivering a halfhearted gesture with my right hand that I don't think Scott, or anyone in the stadium, was buying.

It did not take long to get to the ambulance. The medical personnel had essentially strapped down my neck and entire body, not wanting me to make any unnecessary movements. It was as uncomfortable as it sounds, and I could feel by now that my condition was continuing to go downhill. My heart rate was elevating, and I remember feeling much loopier. Just really dizzy and woozy, and I had a sense it wouldn't be long before I got sick and threw up. It was at this time I started experiencing an incredibly painful headache. This entire time I was still conscious, and Scott was right there by my side, riding with me to the hospital. I was told it was nine minutes from the moment I was struck until I was placed into the ambulance. The ride to the hospital went fast, with the red lights on and siren blaring into a peaceful Iowa afternoon.

I think my state of denial ended somewhere on Third Street on the route to Mercy Medical Center. I was getting worse. I was certain of that. The realities of my symptoms were overtaking my hopeful thoughts of this being a simple concussion. Instead of shaking off my catcher's signs, I had paramedics monitoring my vital signs. Not exactly the plan I had for the day. The whole experience was completely surreal, like dreaming of being in a very bad movie that you can't wake up from.

I do remember that on that brief drive—having no idea where we were going, how long it would take, the severity of my injury, or what was happening next—I collected myself to say a prayer in the back of that ambulance. My heart was racing. I was sweating, feeling claustrophobic. I closed my eyes, searching for inner peace, and focused on these words: *"Lord, be with me. Let me be in my right mind."*

My prayer at that moment was literally that simple, that brief, and that direct. I was coming to grips with the fact that my condition was worse than I'd originally hoped. The end of my prayer coincided with arriving at the hospital. I didn't know how bad my condition was, or what I was in store for next. But I had a feeling I had just said the most important prayer of my life.

The ambulance came to a halt, but the intensity of the situation continued. I was now being pushed through the hospital, still strapped to the stretcher and completely immobile, when I informed the people around me, "I have to throw up." I did. All over my uniform. I remember the unsuspecting nurses being startled. My uniform was a mess, and the nurses asked me if they could cut off my pants. "Yes, go ahead," I told them. It was looking like I might not need them for a while.

While doctors and medical staff were working on figuring out what they were dealing with, I was given a CT scan so they could start finding some answers. I was still tied down, even after throwing up the first time. Yes, I said "first time." I still felt nauseous. I felt like I was going to throw up again, and I did. This time directly on the nurses who were assisting me. I should have felt horrified or embarrassed, but I was in too much pain to feel much of anything else.

Scott had relied on his exceptional training, intelligence, and quick decision making from the time I was injured until I was out of his care in the emergency room. Now that I was in the care of the doctors and nurses, he finally had a moment to collect his thoughts. He knew this was serious, but he told me he hadn't realized how serious it was until a chaplain came over and guided him into a side room. "He started talking to me," Scott said, "and it wasn't really immediate, but it hit me: 'Why is this guy telling me this stuff? Why isn't a doctor here?'"

Scott was able to answer his own question quickly—there was a chance I would die.

• • •

Jenn was with Casen on what up to that point had been an ordinary day at our home in Florida, 1,362 miles away from what was unfolding in the hospital. She had been watching the game online that afternoon, and while Jenn knew I had been struck by a line drive, it wasn't the first time she had seen me get hit by a comebacker on the mound. She told me later that she thought I'd been hit in the shoulder, because it happened so fast and they didn't show a replay right away. But when she saw everybody swarm to me, and the announcers sounded so somber and almost like they were in shock, she started to get nervous. "My reaction then," she said, "was, 'Oh, no. It must have been his head.'"

Jenn's mind was most likely attempting to play the same tricks on her as mine was; thinking and hoping that it was just a concussion. Playing these mind games, convincing yourself in the moment that it might not be as bad as it appears, helps to keep you calm.

Thankfully, Jenn was able to establish contact with the field, and she got a firsthand account of what was going on. I have my friend and teammate Josh Lucas to thank for that. When Josh saw from the bullpen what had happened, and then witnessed the reaction of everyone on the field, he raced into our club-house. Josh grabbed his phone and sent a text to his wife, Whitney, with the cell phone number of our trainer, Scott. Whitney then forwarded Scott's number to Jenn. "I called and texted Scott," Jenn told me, "but by then he was already in the ambulance heading to the hospital with you."

Jenn was able to speak with Scott later, while I was in surgery. Scott informed her that the situation was very serious. Jenn pressed for a little more detail, asking, "Do you think I need to come now? I could change my flight from Friday to Wednesday."

Like all of Scott's actions and decisions that day, he was spot-on with his reply: "You should come now, Jenn," he told her. "I think we need to see if he's going to make it through surgery."

• • •

My dad, Ramon, is a longshoreman and works the overnight shift as a crane operator unloading barges in the port of Long Beach in Southern California. Working those hours allows him to have time in the day to watch my games and support me. He's not the only person working on the ports who follows my career closely. Many of my dad's friends and coworkers are as invested in my success, almost like family, and they take great pride in what I've been able to accomplish in sports and watch most of my games.

My dad told me later that there was one—and only one—instance he remembered where he wasn't able to watch my game online. It was the final game I pitched in 2017. "I mixed up the time for the game," he told me when we discussed it later. "It was an afternoon game, but for some reason I thought it was supposed to be at night. So I was actually at home sleeping. I had no idea what was happening in Iowa."

My dad usually sleeps with his phone and iPad next to him, and the nonstop ringing of his phone alerted him that someone desperately needed to reach him. He woke up and answered his phone, and a buddy of his on the other end of the line asked my dad if he had seen what just happened in the game. He told my dad I was hit by a line drive, and he needed to turn the game on right away.

"His voice, the way he said it, made me really nervous," my dad explained to me. He tuned in to the broadcast and saw at that point I was moving my legs. He figured I'd been hit in the chest. But then the announcers started saying I'd been hit in the head, and he became really worried. He watched as they put me on that stretcher, and then a short time later he got a call from Scott. He said that I was now at the hospital, and a doctor wanted to talk to him.

When I had filled out my emergency contact list, I never imagined the people I put there would ever have to field a call like this. I had listed my dad first, so the doctor used Scott's phone and informed my dad that they'd found bleeding inside my head, and if it continued, he would need him to be available to give authorization to do surgery. "Stay by your phone," the doctor told my dad as he hung up.

"At that point, I just started praying," my dad said. "Fifteen minutes later, they called me back and said they had to go in and operate. The doctor gave me the lowdown on what was about to happen, and then he asked me if I gave them permission to do the surgery."

This was not the first time in his life my dad had experienced the stress of someone very close to him suffering from a medical condition having to do with the brain. Many years before, his own father had suffered a stroke, which required an immediate operation. And when my sister was young, she had contracted meningitis, which resulted in another need for emergency surgery. Now, it was me. He knew from experience how imperative it was that the doctors start the surgery as quickly as possible.

"Yes, please do it immediately," my dad told the doctor. Dad was pretty shaken up at this point, but he knew he had to get to Iowa as fast as he could. He called my brother-in-law and explained to him what had happened. "I told him I couldn't think straight," my dad said. My brother-in-law took charge and booked the plane ticket and made the arrangements for my dad to leave immediately. "At this point," Dad explained, "things were completely out of my hands. So I dropped to my knees and started praying again."

Meanwhile, my mom, Mary, was busy at work that afternoon. She worked as a notary, and she had no way of watching a baseball game online during the day. It was hard for my dad to reach her sometimes, because she simply couldn't be interrupted on the job. This day, my dad was trying to process everything going on and decided not to call my mom until he collected his thoughts and could articulate them. He hoped by then he would have more information to relay.

A short time later he did call my mom, giving her the details he knew, as he raced to the airport to catch his flight. Later, my dad would tell me that his short conversation with my mom was the one and only thing he remembered the rest of the day. "I just knew I had to get there," Dad said. "And I don't remember anything about the trip to Iowa. I don't remember driving to the airport. I don't remember flying in the plane. I can only remember being in the car when I got to Des Moines, going from a rural area into the city and then arriving at the hospital."

• • •

The official box score from our game with the Cubs on May 9, 2017, said it took a total of 2 hours and 26 minutes to play. In parentheses, it listed something else that's rarely, if ever, included in a box score: a 14-minute delay. While I was being prepped for surgery with my life hanging in the balance at the hospital, the game continued, and my teammates were in the fourth inning of a game they would eventually drop 3–1.

Later, I would learn that instead of departing for Memphis and the fifteen-plus-hour drive home immediately after the game, the team bus instead rerouted directly to the hospital, and it remained parked outside while my teammates and coaches waited for updates on my condition. I have no doubt that their prayers and concern at that moment played a role in my ability to survive.

The sound of electric clippers and the painful pulling of my hair caused by an overused shaver were the last things I remembered before the anesthesia took over. As my dad prepared to depart from L.A. and Jenn was being driven to the airport in Orlando, the door to the operating room was closed. My life was now left to the will of God, and in the hands of my surgeons.

CHAPTER 2

FORMING FAITH, MY FAMILY, AND FINDING MY IDENTITY

I am alive by the grace of God. His mercy has allowed me to chase my dreams and strive to become a better version of myself. I wake up each day grateful and humble, hoping to be the best husband, father, and teammate I can be.

When I look back now and think about the severity of my head injury and realize just how bad things could have turned out, I am even more grateful. As strange as it sounds, the injury I suffered was, in some ways, the best thing that has happened in my life. For one thing, it taught me a valuable lesson of just how precious and fragile life is. You naturally explore thoughts like that in the hospital, because you have so much time to think. More importantly, I believe everything—good and bad—happens for a reason, and I now think of my injury as a wake-up call. It showed me just how far I had to go to grow in my journey as a Christian.

For those things, I am thankful. It's humbling to think God can show such mercy to me and not only allow me to survive and come back from my injury, but to become better because of it. This book is the story of my transformation and the spiritual growth that took place during that period; I'm hoping it will be a source of strength and inspiration in some small way for every person who picks up this book and reads it.

Long before that line drive sent me to the hospital in Des Moines, though, I was just another kid in Southern California. I grew up in La Mirada, eighteen miles from downtown Los Angeles, twelve miles from Disneyland, and a world away from a hospital bed in the intensive care unit in the middle of Iowa. My childhood was an idyllic and carefree blur. I played sports year-round, hung with friends, had fun, and lived the awesome So Cal lifestyle. It pretty much fit every cliché of what it's like to grow up in Southern California.

Faith has guided me through a lot of obstacles in my life, and I can thank my dad, Ramon, for that. He started introducing me to Bible passages when I was young and continued throughout my youth. He took me to church, and he instilled a faith in me that I've been able to call on countless times.

While my mom, Mary, was raised Irish-Catholic, she is not, and never has been, a churchgoer. I've never been able to figure out why that is, and it's not something we bring up often because she's made it clear it's something she doesn't feel comfortable talking about. My dad is the opposite. He will talk about anything, including his faith. He raised me as a Christian. What's interesting about my dad is that he was adamant about educating himself as much as he could about every religion he knew of. He understood choosing a faith to follow was a big life decision, and he didn't commit to being a nondenominational Christian until he had researched and taught himself about the differences in all the faiths. He studied the beliefs inherent in the teachings of Buddhism, Islam, Hinduism, Jehovah's Witnesses, Mormonism, and other faiths. Through that research, he said he became closer to God. He challenged his friends of a different faith. He would tell them he knew that their faith believed in certain things, then he would say something like, "Can you show me in the Bible where that is?" He had a strong belief in God's Word, so if what another faith taught couldn't be found in the Bible, he eliminated it. In the end, after ruling out all other faiths, he said it was just him and the Lord left. At that point, he was all in. He was fully committed, and he taught me from and quoted the Bible throughout my childhood.

He has an amazing story of how his belief in Christ was sealed. One day, while he was praying, my dad said he asked God to show him a sign confirming that what he was reading in the Bible was true. He was looking for proof, concrete evidence that would show him he could believe all the words and stories he was reading. It was kind of a bold request, but God apparently felt if my dad was brave enough to ask for such an obvious sign, He might as well give it to him. My dad swears that almost immediately after he asked to see this sign, an earthquake struck. Request granted. The earthquake shook the house and rattled the shelves with such force and fervor that my dad saw it as satisfactory proof, and from that point forward, there was no turning back.

I was baptized when I was eighteen, but the best way to describe my faith back then would be "nonchalant and ignorant." Basically, nonchalant was exactly how I approached almost everything in my life growing up as a laid-back California kid. If you met me back then, you would not walk away saying to yourself, "That is a serious, focused young man with a precise idea of where he's going." Pretty much the opposite. I have an easygoing personality (most of the time), and I wasn't actively seeking ways to grow as a young man of God, which is why I give my dad so much credit for consistently having the presence of the Lord in our house and making sure I was absorbing His teachings.

• • •

Our family consists of my three sisters and my mom and dad, plus me. I was sandwiched between my older sisters, Jackie and Bianca, and my younger sister, Julia. When my mom was pregnant with Julia, I was really hoping to have a baby brother so I would have another boy to play with. Apparently, I even demanded it, and when my parents informed me that my mom was having another girl, I was so angry I started punching my mom's butt! I'd love to be able to say I quickly got over it and accepted the fact that I was going to live in a house full of girls, but I didn't. When Julia was old enough to ride her bike in the backyard, I would use her as target practice, having her ride around in circles as I chucked whatever balls I could find in the garage at her, trying to knock her off her bike. (It wasn't as dangerous as it sounds.) Eventually, I was able to turn my energies to having fun with Julia, jumping on the trampoline and doing other stuff that normal siblings do together.

We have always been a tight-knit family. We did most things as a group, and my sisters and I are very close. They have always been supportive (and, thankfully, forgiving) of me. Looking back, though, there's no doubt being the only boy in the family got me some preferential treatment from my mom. I was a mama's boy growing up, and I had no issues leveraging that power whenever I could. As I mentioned, my dad was a crane operator, and for several years he was also the president of his local union, the ILWU (International Longshore and Warehouse Union). It required not only a lot of late and weird hours on the job at the Port of Los Angeles/Long Beach, but also that he serve as a delegate for the caucus at union conventions around the world. This meant he had to frequently travel to faraway places like Europe, Australia, and Hawaii to conduct union leadership business.

My dad and I have always had an extremely close relationship, and I know a lot of that stems from the countless hours we spent playing and watching sports together when I was growing up. He worked hard, but he never let his job get in the way of coaching me in every sport I played. Whenever possible, he spent time with me in the backyard or in the park, helping me to improve my skills. He was that involved. My biggest fan when I was a kid was my grandpa, my dad's father, who wasn't an actual athlete himself, but he was a huge baseball fan. And because I played baseball, and was pretty good, he showered me with attention and attended almost all of my games. Sadly, he suffered a stroke when I was young, so physically he was paralyzed. He had a hard time moving around and he could barely speak, but he understood what was being said to him pretty well. He died when I was just getting started in my professional career, but when I was in high school, he would always come to my games to watch me play. He would literally cry when he did, because he was so happy for me and got so much satisfaction watching me play the game he loved.

While my mom didn't share my dad's passion for sports and wasn't outside playing catch with me or rebounding shots on the basketball court growing up, she was incredibly supportive of my love for sports even when I was little. She was the one driving me to countless games, practices, and tournaments and then sitting in the stands cheering me on. Many times, my dad couldn't make it because of work, and she was doing it alone. My dad will tell you that it was my mom who carried the load of raising us kids, because his job was too demanding and time-consuming.

Not only was my mom supportive of everything I did, she was and is one of the cooler moms you could hope to have. For example, during my senior year in high school, she asked, "Do you want a letterman's jacket, or something else?"

Since she opened the door with that "something else" line, I figured I'd go for it. "I'd actually rather have a tattoo. I'd never wear a letterman's jacket," I told her.

I let that linger in the air, expecting her to discard the request. But she actually took my request seriously. She let me get a tattoo, and not just any little tattoo on my ankle or shoulder that would be covered by a sock or a sleeve. No, what I had in my mind was a work of art. I got a big, elaborate, complex design that inhabits most of my entire back. The tattoo wasn't cheap. I could probably have purchased several letterman's jackets for what it cost—a whopping $800! It took more than eight hours over multiple sessions for the tattoo artist to complete. My dad found out about it and said, "Are you crazy?" But my mom not only didn't care, she actually came to the tattoo parlor and paid the $800. I'm not sure if she was expecting me to get a tattoo that large, but when I do things, I tend to go all in. I put my heart into the design of this piece of art, and I worked with the tattoo artist to create it. It has a giant cross with interwoven vines running throughout it. I remember that tattoo parlor being in a sketchy part of town, but I knew I was in good hands because the guy who owned the shop was tatted from head to toe, and he even had a tattoo on his eyeball. How could things possibly go wrong with credentials like that? I still have that tattoo and still love it.

. . .

I had a loose, relaxed reputation in high school. But I had a way of morphing into something a little more intense now and then, and it usually happened on the baseball field. I wouldn't say I went from 0 to 100, like the Incredible Hulk, but I could transform into someone much less laid-back when I was playing sports. Baseball can be such an infuriating and frustrating sport, and when you couple that with my short fuse, it could sometimes result in actions that could make people watching say, "This kid has anger issues."

When I was young, I certainly displayed a bad attitude when things didn't work out. I'd throw my helmet and glove and stomp around in a huff. When I think back on it now, I can only imagine the scene I made, and I cringe at the embarrassment I must have caused my parents, coaches, teammates, and everyone else who heard and saw the spectacle. My mom and dad both witnessed it plenty of times in games, and both literally had to get out of their seats, physically restrain me, and pull me off the field when I got out of hand. That's not a good look for a kid, getting yanked from the game by a parent in front of everybody, but that just shows how out of control I could get at times.

Maybe part of it can be rationalized by saying I was so competitive that a fire burned inside of me. That's what my dad believes. (Thanks, Dad.) He will say I held myself to such a high standard on the field that I would naturally hold others to the same standard. Second place wasn't something I was interested in. My dad ingrained in me the importance of winning, so I grew up being very competitive and always wanting to win. My dad's attitude was that they keep score in sports, so you should try to win every time.

All of that might be true on some level, but I can also admit now that it isn't a good excuse for how stupid I would act sometimes. I'd just lose my mind, getting very angry if something went wrong and having it lead to outlandish scenes of immaturity. If I pulled those stunts now, I'd make ESPN's "Not Top 10" list twice a month. Thankfully, God has helped me to mature as an athlete, evolve as a human, and find ways to control any on-the-field outbursts.

I grew up rooting for the Dodgers, mainly because most of my family were big fans. We didn't go to a lot of games in person growing up, but when we did hit a major league park, it would usually be Angels games in Anaheim. My dad would sometimes get free tickets, and their stadium was a much better commute than Dodger Stadium. I loved the exciting feeling I would get seeing the stands glistening in the sun, smelling the freshly cut outfield grass, and getting a glimpse in real life of the players we normally just watched on TV.

Now that I'm a Major League Baseball player, most people assume that my favorite sport as a kid had to have been baseball. That's not true. I enjoyed baseball and played every summer, but once my dad introduced me to football, I fell in love with it. I was even more passionate about basketball than baseball when I was a kid. I had a hoop in my backyard and would shoot for hours almost every day. When I was young, the Lakers were great, winning three titles with Shaquille O'Neal and Kobe Bryant, and during the NBA playoffs I would watch the games on TV through the window as I was shooting hoops in the driveway. When there was a commercial break, I would try to duplicate the moves Kobe had just pulled off, and when the game resumed again I'd put down the ball and continue to peer through the window. If someone had asked me in high school what sport I thought I would play in college, I would have said it would be football for sure, and in a perfect world, I'd try to play baseball as well.

Sports dominated my youth. I seamlessly moved from one season to the next, and when I wasn't on a field or a court, my friends and I would be at the beach as much as we possibly could. Huntington Beach was the closest and best option for us, and it just happened to be one of the greatest beach towns anywhere. My buddies and I would bodysurf and just hang out. I was serious about the things I did growing up, but I had a way of never *taking* those things too seriously. I approached schoolwork as something that was necessary for me to further my athletic career in college. I always found my classes to be more tediously challenging as opposed to mentally challenging, and I knew that I would get out of my studies exactly what I put into them. So I would put the same amount of effort into attaining good grades as I would into skillfully pitching a baseball or throwing a football, and I graduated from high school with a GPA near 4.0.

I had a happy-go-lucky personality. The great family life I grew up with allowed me to play sports and have fun and not think much about my long-term future. If someone had asked me what I would do with my life if I wasn't a baseball player or athlete, I wouldn't have had an answer for them. The truth was, not only did I *not* know what I would do, I had absolutely no plan. I couldn't imagine a life that didn't include sports in some way, and I knew college was the next stop.

There are two glamorous universities with campuses within an hour of our house: UCLA, where I had literally visualized myself starring in football in the fall and baseball in the spring, and USC.

Throughout my athletic career, there has been a running theme of being told I'm not good enough to do something or play at a certain level. While some people might have found this disheartening and aggravating, it didn't bother me because I never believed or even thought twice about it.

I attended summer football camp at both schools when I was developing into what I thought was a pretty good quarterback prospect. At that time, Pete Carroll had turned the University of Southern California Trojans into a college football power. They had a star-studded group of highly recruited superstars at almost every position and an A-list fan base that included the who's who in Los Angeles. Across town in Westwood, at UCLA, former Bruins star Rick Neuheisel was the head coach of a less talented team, but one that was certainly on the rise and still pretty good. At each camp, I was determined to convince the coaches through my play that they had found their next quarterback. All they had to do was put a scholarship in front of me and I would have signed it on the spot. I thought I competed well against the other quarterback competition. I was completing the most passes and shredding the opposing defenses with ease. While I thought I was showing I could be the next Tom Brady, Matt Leinart, or Troy Aikman and take either of these teams to the Rose Bowl, I don't think Carroll and Neuheisel were aware I was there. I certainly don't blame them personally, because they were searching for the 6′5″ prospects who looked like they came out of central casting for how a star QB should appear, while I was a lanky 6′3″, 185-pound kid slinging the rock.

In the end, instead of the easy route of signing with one major university located in Southern California—which was what I thought would be a short path to a professional league— I would instead start down one of the most winding roads you could possibly take to a big league career. My journey had just begun.

CHAPTER 3

COLLEGE LIFE; FUTURE WIFE

My journey to the majors has been unique. In fact, I might be the only player in big league history who has attended four colleges in four states, had one scholarship yanked, had one big-money signing bonus rescinded, and been declared ineligible by the NCAA. Through all of that, I have also been lucky enough to be selected four different times, by four different teams, in four Major League Baseball drafts. That's not what you lie in bed dreaming about when you are eleven years old. My path to professional baseball was a winding, pothole-filled, roller-coaster ride of ups and downs that would ultimately test my perseverance, patience, confidence, and faith. And, like the day I was hit in the head by that one line drive, I wouldn't change a single thing about it.

It started with my ignorance on what most young athletes would consider the best day of their lives. It was the end of my senior year in high school. I was sitting at a table with my teammates at our end-of-season baseball banquet when I looked down at my phone to see a phone number on the screen I had never seen before. I answered the phone and the voice on the other end of the line said, "Hi, Daniel. My name is Jake Wilson of the Tampa Bay Rays, and we just drafted you in the twenty-fourth round of the major league draft."

"What?" I replied as I walked outside to find a quieter spot. "Could you say that again?"

"Yeah. It's Jake Wilson of the Tampa Bay Rays. We just drafted you in the twenty-fourth round of the major league draft. We'll contact you in the next day or two and go over things."

"Okay. Cool," I calmly replied.

I walked back into the banquet room and said to my dad, "I just got drafted." Now keep in mind, I had no idea when the draft was, and I definitely didn't know it was going on that day. I sat down thinking to myself, "That was kind of cool," but another part of me was saying, "What just happened?"

When I think about it now, knowing what was to come and how difficult it would be, I realize it's a good thing I was essentially clueless concerning the process. If I had known what the path to professional baseball looked like, I am not sure I would have traveled down that road.

It sure started out promising. My high school coaches had me attend a showcase that dozens of college coaches and scouts attended. They would evaluate the players and see if there was Division I talent worth recruiting. Not surprisingly, I went to the showcase having no idea what it was. My dad was watching the scene around me as I pitched off the mound. He later told me coaches would watch their radar guns, and early on, my fastball was being clocked in the mid-80s. The coaches weren't very impressed, but then the velocity started ticking up. I hit 88 mph on the gun. A couple of pitches later it registered 89. I followed that with a fastball that clocked 90 mph, and my dad said at that point everyone watching me throw started writing on their clipboards. Whatever I did led the University of Arizona to be interested in signing me, and that was where I went for my freshman year. I thought it was going to be the perfect place for me too. A substantial part of my education was being paid for through my scholarship, and it was close enough to Southern California that my family would be able to see some games. The warm weather year-round would be ideal for a pitcher like me, and the Wildcats were in the marquee Pac-10 Conference (now the Pac-12), one of the best baseball leagues in the entire country. I didn't have many other offers to choose from, and none at a major Division I university, so when my dad and I went on our visit to the campus and the coaches told us everything we wanted to hear, we were blown away. I thought it would be the ideal spot for me, and I couldn't have been more excited. It turned out I couldn't have been more wrong.

It was a few minutes into my very first bullpen session, in my first practice, in the fall of my freshman year that I realized the head coach watching and talking to me now was not sounding like the same person who had recruited me just a few months earlier. That coach told me everything I wanted to hear and made it seem like I would be a positive addition to the team. Now he was standing on the mound next to me with an annoyed look on his face as I struggled with my control and tried to throw strikes. When I didn't, he screamed at me loud enough for anyone near us to hear it. He was cutting into me in front of my teammates, and as I would learn as the year progressed, it was the opening act of an entire season of intense criticism. The hard part for me was figuring out why he had changed into this version of a coach who essentially had no use for me. I thought it might be his style of motivation. The approach must work with some players, because the coach had won two College World Series titles, so it's not like he wasn't successful. Maybe it was my laid-back attitude that could be misinterpreted as indifference. My dad definitely thinks that is the case, and he says people have misjudged me this way for years. I can be hard to read based on a first impression. I'm low-key, and to some people that might seem like I don't care, which is the complete opposite of how things really are. I care a great deal. But all I knew at that moment was the coach wasn't a fan of the way I was throwing.

The harsh tone started early on and it continued, and it led me to believe I was a marked man among my teammates. Nobody wants to hang around the guy constantly getting yelled at, and I felt at times guys would distance themselves from me, thinking I might be toxic. It's human nature to do that, especially in a sports setting. It's not like I could ask the coach what he didn't like about me or why he seemed to have it out for me. I was a lowly freshman. I wasn't in the regular rotation. I had no reason to believe I was part of the coach's long-term plans based on the intense, negative feedback I was receiving. And he never let up. I remember running onto the field every single day before practice, just trying to warm up, and the coach would always be right there, yelling at me, "The bullpen is the safest place. The bullpen is the safest place!" I guess he was informing me and a couple of fellow pitchers that we had it easier than other players because we were only relief pitchers for the team. However, it's not like we were hiding out there and taking naps. The verbal agitation was nonstop, and it became demoralizing. Still, even with insults cutting deep every time I'd hear them, I wasn't completely broken yet. I felt I was pitching well enough in practice to at least earn some innings in a game once the season started. I might have been a little delusional, but I had to find something positive to hold on to.

Things progressively got worse. We were scheduled to take a road trip to Southern California, a weekend visit to Los Angeles to play UCLA, and I was looking forward to seeing my friends and family, maybe even pitching in a game. The coach squashed that thought by not even taking me on the trip. It was the only conference road trip I didn't go on.

After talking to other players, I came to believe that this was just the coach's style. It was his method of motivation, but it left me standing on the practice field one day in March of my freshman season, unable to hold back the tears that were streaming down my face after another tongue-lashing. By then, I was completely broken, yet the admonishment continued, and it could and would come at any time, in any place. No setting was too awkward or off-limits for him to remind me that I wasn't the right fit for the program. On our trip to Oregon, we lost two of the three games to the Ducks, including the final game of the series. After the game, the entire team showered together in the locker room before heading to the bus, which would take us to the airport for the flight back to Tucson. At this point in the season, I hadn't even played in an actual game in more than two months, and as I walked into the shower, the coach saw me. My mere presence just set him off. "I should have never brought you on this trip! You don't deserve to be here!" he screamed as we both stood there in the shower. Completely naked. By this point, I'd had enough, and I started yelling right back at him. Here we are, a coach and a freshman barking at each other so intensely our catcher had to play peacemaker and calm us down.

I ended up appearing in just three innings the entire season, and because of those three innings, I lost my ability to redshirt. This would have meant that I could have four more years of eligibility, but because I'd pitched those three innings, it counted as a full season. After everything that transpired, you might think I had my bags packed on the last day of school and a transfer already figured out. But I had no intention of quitting. Our last game of the season was followed by the end-of-year meetings, and I walked into the coach's office fully expecting to get berated and reminded yet again how I didn't belong. Surprisingly, the opposite occurred. The coach was back in recruiting mode, calmly explaining how the team was looking for me to come back as a weekend starter the next season. He talked about how he valued me as one of the best pitchers returning. "We're going to need you," he commented, one of the few times I had heard something positive. He filled me up with everything I wanted to hear. I went back to California to play summer ball to improve, thinking I would be in Tucson for my sophomore season. But a short time later, I received a call from the pitching coach, delivering me one final indignity: "I wanted you to know that we are not renewing your scholarship. Would you like us to help you find another college?"

"Nope," I replied. I hung up the phone, buried my head in my pillow, and let out a muffled scream. That was all I needed to put my University of Arizona experience behind me. I moved on to prayer. Two days later the word was out, and my phone started ringing with better news as coaches were calling to invite me to play for their programs. I soon realized I would have a major decision to make.

Considering how nonexistent my impact was in my freshman year, I was surprised at how many calls I received, and how many other schools were interested in me—and not just baseball coaches. My dad was reaching out to schools and telling them I was available to play football, too, and I received full-scholarship offers from Kansas and New Mexico State, as well as offers from smaller schools like UC Davis. Most of them were going to let me play football and baseball if I chose to. My dad and I gave it a lot of thought, and we felt the smartest plan would be for me to find a junior college with a great baseball program that was close to home. In order for me to go back to a Division I school, I would have to play at a junior college for one season. I initially chose Golden West College in Huntington Beach, but two weeks later I changed my mind and decided to attend Cypress College. The community college in Cypress was a short drive from my home and was known for having a roster filled with players who wanted to get drafted or transfer back to a Division I school. Basically, it was for people like me, looking for a second chance and a soft landing after a rough experience. Cypress was the most logical choice for me on every level, so I called the coaches at Golden West to tell them that I had changed my mind. They did not take the news very well. After getting screamed at by them for a minute or so, I turned my attention to getting my athletic career back on track.

College baseball players are mostly eligible to be drafted by major league teams after their senior year in high school, following their junior year in a four-year college, or any time in junior college. My one season at Cypress went well enough that I was being contacted by scouts throughout the season, and this time I was not naive about the process like I was in high school. I had a good perspective on how baseball's new draft signing bonus system worked, so I informed teams that I would sign for a minimum of $200K. That dollar amount turned off a few teams, and it meant that I wasn't selected in the first two days of the draft. On the third day, the Cincinnati Reds took a chance on me, selecting me in the thirty-eighth round, where signing bonuses were tiny compared to the money being offered for players picked in the first couple of rounds. I was flattered to be chosen, but my mind was set on finding school number three following draft number two.

After prayer and thought, I decided to adopt a more businesslike approach to the upcoming recruiting process than I had in the past. The one school that showed the most interest in me and had scholarship money available was the University of Houston. They made no pie-in-the-sky promises to me, which I really liked and found refreshing. I knew with a coach just starting his second season, I was in a situation where I controlled my own fate. If I had serious aspirations to be drafted again after my junior year at Houston, I would need to be a weekend pitcher for the Cougars, and, frankly, I was excited and ready for the challenge. I packed my bags for Texas with my goals and priorities set, an open mind, and my faith intact.

I arrived in Houston during the summer and trained with my new team for a couple of months before school started. Once the season began, I was slated as the Friday night starter, the most prominent role for a college pitcher. Our Saturday starting pitcher was Austin Pruitt, another future major leaguer who pitched much better than I did that season, but because I threw harder, with my velocity in the low 90s, I had the honor of pitching the Friday night game. My problem was that I was inconsistent. I would be lights-out and unhittable in one game, then struggle to find the zone. The coaching staff was supportive and had a lot of trust in me, and they rode this roller coaster with me through the ups and downs. They took a different approach in comparison to the coaches I'd had in the past. When the season ended, I was feeling confident that I would be drafted, but I had no illusions I would be going in the first round.

The Cubs eventually selected me in the fourteenth round, and because I had a better understanding of how the draft process worked, and a little bit of leverage because I had the option of returning to school for my senior season, I asked the Cubs for two things in our negotiations: a $100,000 signing bonus and an agreement that the club would pay for me to finish college when I was able to return—a typical college junior sign that fell out of the top ten rounds. They agreed to both. It was an amazing blessing and I was so grateful. I took a picture with the scout and posted the details of my upcoming professional baseball career on Twitter.

In case you haven't noticed a theme yet, I didn't have a lot of fairy-tale endings in college, and this would be no exception. Another disappointing setback was around the corner; another opportunity to test my faith in God to help me navigate yet another unorthodox and trying situation.

Believing I was about to become a professional athlete with a little bit of money in my bank account, I immediately departed for Mesa, Arizona, where the Cubs spring training facility is. I was set to undergo a routine physical and an MRI on my pitching arm, just like every player the team had just drafted. After going through the battery of tests with no complications, the team trainers told me I could sleep in the next morning, since my physical exams were completed. But the next morning, there was a knock on my door. "Hi, Daniel. We need you to come in for another MRI," the clubbie told me. "Why?" I asked him. "You just do," he replied.

So off I went, the only pitcher asked to undergo three MRIs— it was not the kind of team record I was looking to set. After the additional screening, I received a call the following morning from someone with the Cubs, informing me that they were not going to sign my contract because they didn't like the nerve placement in my right arm. I went numb, completely stunned and caught off guard by this worst-case scenario. The person on the call continued to explain, but I wasn't even listening at this point. All I knew was it was yet another setback. Just one more obstacle I would have to find a way to overcome.

I have never been a person who feels sorry for himself. I don't get overly excited at good news, and I take bad news in stride, even this gut punch. I had to do something, so my next move was to call my coaches at Houston, asking if they would allow me to come back to school for my senior year. They told me I could come back, but the athletic department compliance officers knew about the Twitter post and my offer from the Cubs. They were obligated to report it to the NCAA. My short-term and long-term future was in limbo. To Houston's credit, the school backed me completely, arguing with the NCAA and pleading my case that I should be allowed to play my senior season. I wrote an essay to explain the situation that I hoped would allow the NCAA to see my side. I re-enrolled in school at Houston and worked out the entire fall on my own—I wasn't even able to join my teammates in any training sessions—as I waited for a ruling by the NCAA. Houston had already given away my scholarship to a new player, so my dad and I went into debt and paid for the fall semester out-of-pocket. The ruling finally came in mid-December, and the verdict was not what I wanted to hear. I was ineligible. And I wouldn't be able to play at any other NCAA school either. If I wanted to play for a professional team, my only option would be to sign a free agent contract and basically try out. I didn't want to do that. I had zero leverage. But I never considered quitting…never. I didn't blame God, I didn't freak out, and I didn't think my baseball career was over.

My college years really were a wild ride, and my faith mirrored how things were going in my life. When things were going well, I wasn't reading my Bible as much as I should have. I let my faith slip. And when times got tough, the only thing I knew to fall back on for strength was my Bible and my faith. It's a sad but true fact that when there are few challenges to overcome, most people drift from God's Word and their faith, instead of thanking Him for the smooth ride. But when you stumble or get humbled, that is when you come running back to the Lord. I try to explain to people that you can't do it all and overcome every challenge on your own—you just can't. Every time you think you don't need God, He will find a way to humble you, because that's His way of showing He cares. I've learned that the hard way many times in my life. I wish I knew back then what I know now, but falling down is just part of maturing. God has always been there to pick me up.

My unconventional, wandering path to a professional baseball career would have to locate another landing spot. I needed to find another college that could accommodate the limitations I was facing. Thankfully, I had my faith to fall back on during another uncertain time, and a lifeline fell out of the sky and into my life. God's favor was on full display, and it resulted in a decision that changed the course of my life.

• • •

My pitching coach at the University of Houston had coached the pitching coach at an obscure school in Florida that I had never heard of and that played at a level of college athletics I was not even aware of. The school was Embry-Riddle Aeronautical University in Daytona Beach. It was a college most known for flight training, not training professional baseball players. But it was an NAIA (National Association of Intercollegiate Athletics) school, not NCAA (National Collegiate Athletic Association), and that meant I would be eligible to play right away. And the school was committed to baseball. That appealed to me. The team was really good, ranked third nationally, and at that point in my career, I knew it didn't matter where I pitched. If I had enough talent to be a major league prospect, teams would find me like they always had. I was heading to Florida and a school called Embry-Riddle to take one final shot at chasing my dream. Failing was not an option.

I arrived on campus with what I thought was an ironclad game plan. I was locked in on one thing: baseball. I wanted no distractions, and that meant I would be saying no to dating, and girls in general. There wasn't room in my life at the time to even consider anything but baseball. The decision was easy because men made up 77 percent of Embry-Riddle's student population. There were dudes everywhere. I was committed to making sure nothing would stop me from staying focused and girlfriend-free, and I'm proud to say I was 100 percent successful in that effort. Until my first class, on my very first day of school.

I literally knew only one person on the baseball team, and coincidentally, he was also in the same class as me. He sat down and I took the seat next to him. As fate would have it, an empty seat remained open on the other side of me, and a beautiful girl walked into the room and filled that seat. I glanced around the room, making sure someone wasn't playing a joke on me. This kind of thing didn't happen to me. I usually wasn't this lucky.

In fact, this had *never* happened to me. The prettiest girl on campus walked in and sat down right next to me in a seat that just happened to be open. By chance, she knew my teammate, so they began talking and catching up. I eventually joined the conversation and introduced myself to her. While I thought she was incredibly beautiful, and I was certainly intrigued, I tried to remain calm and keep my plan intact. No girls. My first class on my first day was not the time to waver! Within a couple of days we'd gotten to know each other a little better, and she invited me to her apartment for dinner. I remember the moment I walked in vividly; she had Christian music playing in the background and the smell of an amazing meal drifting in from the kitchen. I didn't know it at the time, but I had just found the last girl I'd ever fall for.

I pitched well in my one and only season at Embry-Riddle, and there was little doubt I would be drafted. There were scouts at nearly every game, watching me when I pitched. The team showing me the most interest all along was the St. Louis Cardinals, specifically their scout Charlie Gonzalez. Charlie aggressively pursued me, calling me almost every day. He called me more than my entire family combined, checking in on me and asking me questions. He had this unusual tendency to not say good-bye when he was done talking. He would just hang up, while I'd be on the other end, going, "Hello? Charlie? You there?"

When draft day arrived in June 2014, a number of teams called me, and I told them that I was asking for a modest signing bonus of $30,000 or $40,000. All I wanted was enough to pay off my college loans, play baseball debt-free, and not be completely broke as I started my professional career. One team called and told me they would agree to that, but then Charlie called and said, "We're going to take you in the ninth round."

Knowing the Cardinals were drafting before that team called, I pleaded for Charlie to pass on me. "Don't take me; don't take me," I told him. But the Cardinals didn't care about the promised bonus from that certain team. They selected me in the ninth round of the 2014 MLB draft. Just like Charlie said they would. Being drafted after your senior season in college means you can say so long to big signing bonuses. What I had worked out with the Blue Jays was rare. Teams know you have no other options, so they can offer $1,000 or so up front and there's nothing a player can do about it. The Cardinals were very gracious and paid me a $5,000 bonus. I may not have known it at the time, but that five grand, added to the fact that I had also found my future wife, essentially meant I had just hit the lottery.

CHAPTER 4

BIG LEAGUE DREAMS; MINOR LEAGUE REALITIES

Living on a yacht docked on the coast of the ritzy Florida city of Palm Beach sounds glamorous. When the AC is broken, your monthly take-home pay is less than $1,000, and the dew-point level matches the outside temperature on another hot and muggy Sunbelt night, it's not as awesome as it sounds. Ah, the life of a minor leaguer. I experienced at first hand everything you've heard about coming up in the lower minor leagues. Long bus rides, basic facilities, creative dining options. It's a rite of passage for players chasing a Major League Baseball dream, and I'm sure my situation was similar to what others have gone through. But I had a few unique twists.

My journey began in a charming college town smack-dab in the middle of Pennsylvania. The town of State College is home to not only the iconic Penn State Nittany Lions, but also the lesser-known State College Spikes, my first minor league team. I learned during my short tenure there that the nickname "Spikes" is not a reference to the footwear of baseball players. It signifies a young white-tailed deer whose undeveloped horns are just small *spikes* poking out of the deer's head. It's meant to symbolize a young baseball player hoping to develop into a major leaguer, and that's a pretty good analogy for where I was in my professional life as a baseball player.

Jenn and I went to California to visit my family after the season at Embry-Riddle concluded and I was drafted by the Cardinals. It was the fourth time I had been drafted, and I knew there was not going to be a fifth, so I boarded a plane within days and launched my professional career before another bizarre occurrence could postpone it.

The Spikes are the Cardinal's short-season Class-A affiliate. Their season runs just three months—June, July, and August. During the time I played for the team, all the players stayed with host families in the community so we wouldn't have to rent apartments. We ended up winning the championship that season, and by late summer, I was more than ready for a break. I had thrown over one hundred innings during my senior college season in Florida, and then fifty-four more with the Spikes, so my arm was fried.

"How would you like to work for my grandpa this off-season?" Jenn asked me shortly after the season ended. I had nothing but time and no other jobs lined up, so that sounded great. Her grandpa owns a successful construction company and he gave me a marketing job, where my main role was hosting open houses in model homes on weekends. It paid more than my professional baseball job, including my signing bonus! Being able to earn some money meant the only thing to worry about was getting ready for the next season. I didn't have an official off-season workout regimen from the team to follow. Because I was a low-level prospect, it was up to me to make sure I was improving and getting ready for spring training, and I had one goal that fall and winter: get stronger. I was on a mission to make sure that when spring training began, I was starting with a full-season club and not going back to the short-season team. I knew I needed to bulk up to do that. When there were no house hunters to speak with on my job, I spent the downtime on YouTube watching videos to learn the proper way to deadlift and bench-press. I wanted to get as strong as I possibly could, and through my self-taught training regimen, I was able to increase the max speed of my fastball from 93 to 97 mph.

I knew spring training for the Cardinals was in Florida, but I wasn't exactly sure where until I got the letter telling me to report to camp in Jupiter. Jupiter turned out to be a beautiful, affluent city on the southeast coast of Florida that has been home to Michael Jordan, Tiger Woods, and many other successful former and current athletes and personalities. It was a blessing that spring training was only about two and a half hours away from New Smyrna Beach, where Jenn grew up and currently lived. We saw each other throughout that off-season, and she was able to visit me in Jupiter a few times too. I had saved a few bucks, packed on some muscle, and reported to camp in 2015 ready to make a name for myself. It was my first professional spring training, my first chance to show the Cardinals organization what I could do. Over the course of the next eight months, there would be many more firsts, including one that would put a strain on my relationship with Jenn and make both of us wonder if it would last.

There are a lot of things to learn when you are a young baseball player navigating the minor leagues for the first time. Especially for someone like me. I was what they call a "senior sign."

That meant I signed after my senior year in college—the lowest end of the totem pole for players drafted. My signing bonus was just $5,000, which meant the team had invested very little in me, and I would have to earn every opportunity I would get. Nothing was going to be handed to me. I was one of the few young players at spring training who had a car, which made me a popular guy. I lived in the team hotel with one roommate, and we would pile four players into my car and arrive at the ballpark as early as we could to get a jump on our day. That meant eating breakfast in the clubhouse, which featured a menu that usually consisted of powdered eggs, unsalted fake bacon, and oatmeal, which had the texture and taste of cardboard. For my pregame meal, I would get creative and put together a concoction from what the team made available in the clubhouse. I would spread peanut butter and jelly on an uncooked tortilla, add a hand-ful of goldfish snacks to give it extra texture and a dry, cheesy flavor, then roll it up and devour it. What it may have lacked in nutritional value and taste, it made up for in being affordable. Most decisions you make when playing low-level minor league ball are economical. At the forefront of my decision making was to spend as little money as I could.

Since I didn't have any money to eat out, I decided that if I wanted access to better food options, I would have to work my way up to a higher level with the Cardinals as fast as I could. After several weeks of spring training in sunny Florida, I was told I would start the season playing for the Cardinals Single-A team, the Peoria Chiefs. It would be my first exposure to early springtime weather in the Midwest. In other words, freezing-cold conditions. And we opened the season on the road in Wisconsin. It was the coldest weather I had ever experienced. I wish I could say I was mentally and physically prepared for it, but I wasn't. One of the jobs of a starting pitcher who wasn't playing was to chart pitches from the stands during the game. When it was my turn, I sat on the uncomfortable metal bleachers wearing my full baseball uniform underneath all of the regular clothes I wore to the ballpark. I'd try anything I could to stay warm, and nothing worked. Wisconsin cold was new to me. Growing up in Southern California, and playing college ball in Arizona, Houston, and Florida, did not prepare me for this type of bitter chill.

I had no control over the weather. But one thing I could control was how hard I threw the baseball when I was on the mound, and I made sure to put my newfound strength from the off-season weight training into every pitch. I wasn't going to overthink anything on the mound. My strategy was to rear back and throw hard.

Another thing I had no control over as a player was the mechanical state of the buses we spent a lot of time in. Single-A ball is a matter of survival in some regards. The bus rides were constant, long, and one of the most challenging aspects of minor league life. We'd have close to thirty people on the bus when we hit the road. There's a pecking order of who sits where, with the front of the bus occupied by the manager, pitching coach, hitting coach, strength coach, and team trainer. They each would have their own individual row to themselves, too, which meant the players had to cram into the rest of the bus. We had a rule that if the city we were playing in was three and a half hours away or less, we would bus back and forth to that city for each game. Three and a half hours there, and the same monotonous trip back. Then wake up and do it all over again. If the city was four hours away, we would stay the night in that city and not have to make the daily commute. The places we played were remote outposts, oftentimes in the middle of nowhere, which meant if the bus broke down, there was nothing to do but hope for the best and wait for help. We were in the Western Division of the Midwest League, with games in cities like Cedar Rapids, Burlington, and Clinton in Iowa; Beloit and Appleton in Wisconsin; and the Quad Cities, Peoria, and Kane County in Illinois. On one trip returning from a game, we were two hours from Peoria when our bus broke down. Luckily, there was a church we could walk to, and we waited it out for four hours there before a replacement bus arrived. Taller guys like me were seldom able to get comfortable on the bus. I remember always contorting my body in some crooked position, straining and turning to try to find a spot that could provide a little relief before half of my body went numb. It was a miserable experience much of the time, but a necessary evil for every player who's done it.

What kept me going through all the long rides, unfamiliar weather, and bad meals was an inner drive to be the best I could be. I know that sounds cliché and simple, but there was really no other option. If I pitched well, got noticed, stayed healthy, and took advantage of every opportunity I had to impress a coach or scout or the Cardinals farm director, I would move up another level and get a chance to do it all over again. There were no shortcuts or magic formulas. An advantage I had that not everyone else could claim was the support of my family. I also had my Christian faith. The combination of all those things paid off, because after a few months pitching in Peoria, I was called up in 2015 to the Cardinals high Class-A affiliate in Palm Beach on the Fourth of July. The day I received that promotion was one of the happiest days of my life. Even though there was just a marginal upgrade in competition at the level I would be playing at, there was a night-and-day difference in intangibles. For starters, the longest bus ride we'd take would be approximately three and a half hours, and if we rode that long we'd always stay the night in the city we played in. It might not sound like much, but to a minor leaguer with no money toiling in Single-A ball, it was equivalent to being upgraded from the middle seat in the back row of a regional airline plane to a window seat in an empty row of a jumbo jet.

There was another perk of playing for a Cardinals affiliate in Palm Beach that I was grateful for that summer: access to the big league club's spring training facilities. The fields were kept in pristine condition and the locker rooms were modern and spacious. Financially, every day was still a grind. My pay didn't change noticeably with the promotion to Palm Beach. I was still grossing roughly $1,200 per month, which meant on my payday every two weeks, a few hundred dollars would be deposited into a checking account that seemed to always be running on fumes. One thing that took some sting out of the low pay was the proximity to Jenn. The odds of my playing minor league baseball close to her were almost nonexistent, but here I was, less than two hundred miles from her hometown. One of the toughest things for any young couple to cope with is being apart, and now that was less of an issue for us. It was a blessing for our relationship, and so was the generosity of Jenn's family, which saved me money I didn't have at this stage in my career. Jenn's grandpa offered to sail his yacht up to Palm Beach and dock it there for me to live on during the remainder of the season. "Yacht" would be the *technical* description of the boat. There's no doubt my teammates thought it was cool, and it was an incredible gesture by Jenn's grandpa, but it wasn't the type of yacht you'd see in the South of France during the Cannes Film Festival. The air-conditioning broke down at least four times, but I didn't want to seem ungrateful, so instead of complaining, I learned to deal with it. On nights the AC was broken, it would be impossible to sleep inside, so I sucked it up, climbed to the roof of the yacht, and hoped for a cool breeze as I batted mosquitoes and tried to get some sleep.

I was happy to be in Florida, and my philosophy was that I had a job to do. I couldn't let long bus rides, broken AC units, and questionable cuisine get in the way of my mission. I kept the same pitching philosophy I had in Peoria after I moved up: It was my fastball versus the hitter. My goal for the season was to dominate, and I felt I'd done that during the early weeks in Peoria. Once I got to Palm Beach, I pitched well, but in late summer I felt a soreness in my shoulder that continued until the club had to shut me down for the season in August. I spent the second half of August sitting in the stands, sweating as I charted pitches, shedding layers of clothes as quickly as I had been adding layers a few months earlier. Logging every pitch thrown was frustrating. I longed to be out there on the mound myself, but in order to do that, I had to get whatever was wrong with my shoulder straightened out. Thanks to my agent, Brian Grieper, I was able to accomplish just that. Brian connected me with Eric Cressey, a guru of sports performance with a master's degree in kinesiology who has worked with over a hundred professional athletes, including superstar pitchers Max Scherzer, Corey Kluber, and Noah Syndergaard. Luckily, Eric was based in Florida, so I was able to take what I learned from him and incorporate it into my personal workouts that off-season.

Finding a leading shoulder strength and conditioning coach for me is just one of the ways Brian has helped not only in my career, but in all aspects of my life. Some people say that a great agent becomes like family, and that's what Brian is to me. He's been there for me since day one, and he was at many games when I pitched in Palm Beach. He knew exactly what to watch for in my performance, and after the games, we would get together to have dinner and Brian would have spot-on evaluations of what was and wasn't working for me on the mound. I appreciated that for sure, as well as another generous thing Brian did for me after games. He would always take me to get a good meal, and every single time he would pay for it. It would often be the best meal I had all week, a real treat, and I was thankful he did pay because there's no way I could have. Some habits are hard to break, because even now, Brian won't let me pick up a check when we go out.

Brian tells a great story of how he and I connected. Before he met me, he had a relationship with Charlie Gonzalez, the scout for the Cardinals who signed me out of Embry-Riddle. "I found a guy who has a million-dollar arm that I'm going to sign for about five or ten thousand dollars," Charlie told Brian. Brian tried to get the name of this prospect from Charlie, but he wouldn't tell him, fearing Brian would try to drive up the signing bonus. Eventually, Charlie caved and Brian introduced himself to my dad and me. Soon after that we signed with him. It was one of the best decisions I've made.

Great agents just have an innate ability to know what needs to be done. Brian even helped me with the paperwork to defer my college loans from Embry-Riddle. "This is where you'll want to fill out this document and send it to the address on the top of the form," I remember Brian telling me, pointing to the form he had downloaded and printed. He facilitated the whole thing and guided me through it. I had a pretty viable reason at the time for requesting the deferral: I was broke. I couldn't have paid the loans back at that time even if I'd wanted to, but the deferral allowed me to pay off those balances a few years later.

I approached the 2015 off-season convinced I would start the 2016 season in Double-A, another rung closer to pitching in the big leagues. I had a short-term goal in February when I reported to my first big league camp with the Cardinals at their spring training facility in Jupiter; I planned to not give up any runs. I was in the best shape of my life, my shoulder was strong, and I felt like I could pitch all day. You couldn't tell by my first Grapefruit League game, though. I pitched horribly against a college team in my debut. I was awful, walking batters, throwing wild pitches, and looking like someone who had no business even being on the field. After that debacle, I pitched against major league teams in my next four outings that spring, and I didn't give up a single run.

One thing that's said about the game of baseball is it has a way of humbling you. I learned that firsthand, when I was sent to minor league spring training halfway through camp, leaving the big league facilities, players, coaches, and amenities behind. Although it was shocking and frustrating because I was pitching well, I convinced myself it wasn't personal. It was more of a predetermined decision, since I wasn't going to be starting the season on the major league roster anyway. I was a senior sign, which meant I had to create my own breaks.

The news of being sent to finish spring training with the minor leaguers didn't really bother me, but a short time later I was told I would start the season in Palm Beach, Single-A ball again, and I was irate. I felt I had pitched well all spring and deserved to be in Double-A, and it was incredibly frustrating. I was less equipped to handle moments like that back then. I had not fully grasped the concept that God ultimately controlled my path, so I pridefully tried to make myself feel better by being angry. But God stepped in and blessed me with an amazing set of circumstances just two days before the season was to start. One of the pitchers on the Double-A roster had to undergo Tommy John surgery, opening a roster spot for me with the Double-A club in Springfield, Missouri. This was monumental. I could close the Single-A chapter of my life as my career arc brought me to the "Queen City of the Ozarks."

My new team opened the 2016 season in San Antonio, a sixteen-hour bus ride from Springfield. Due to the timing of my promotion, I was able to avoid the drive and take a flight straight to Texas. Playing in Springfield taught me just how big the state of Texas is. After that season-opening series in San

Antonio, we went straight to Corpus Christi to continue the road trip. Corpus Christi is located in the most southern part of Texas, over two hundred miles south of Houston. From there, it's eighteen hours of asphalt back to Springfield. Our team traveled on two buses, one with sleeper beds and a normal bus (no sleeper beds) for the younger players on the team. As someone new to the team, that's the bus I would ride, and as I've already mentioned, in order to get rest, we'd do anything possible to find a comfortable position to sleep. That often meant lying on the floor of the bus as it cruised along one of the many state highways on the eleven-hundred-mile trip. I'll never forget what happened on one of the horrendously long stretches that had us traveling through the night. I found a spot on the floor to crash for a few hours and I woke up just as the bus pulled into an IHOP. On top of being stiff and sore from the modified sleeping arrangement, I was soaking wet. It wasn't hot enough inside the bus where I would have sweat through my clothes in the early morning, so something wasn't right. There was a cooler on the floor right next to me, and my first instinct was to look inside the cooler to see if it had leaked water. It hadn't. Oh, how I wish that had been the case. My mind started drifting into other more likely, less desirable scenarios. Situated on the other side of me was a teammate, also sleeping on the floor, and he was wet too. You don't need many more clues to figure out the source of the leak. He had lost control of a bodily function, and in the process drenched the floor, himself, and everything else located downhill from him (i.e., me). There's no handbook on how to handle this shock. I didn't know whether to try to fight him or just act like nothing happened and get cleaned up. "God, what is going on?" I remember saying to myself as I tried to calm down.

There are a lot of difficult aspects of minor league living—the emotional swings of playing, being away from home or family for the first time, or simply finding a way to get yourself to sleep on long bus rides—and they often lead players to self-medicate. Alcohol seems to be the drug of choice for most, and I have seen its damaging effects both on and off the field. The way I handled these trying circumstances that are so natural in the minor leagues was to just deal with them. There was no other option. I hadn't yet experienced the comforts of traveling as a major league player, so for me, I didn't feel I was missing anything. I didn't know any better. A long bus ride in Double-A beat a long bus ride in Single-A. I tried to use every passing mile of farmland as fuel to hopefully accelerate my rise in the Cardinals farm system. Waking up on the floor of a bus with my clothes wet with someone else's urine certainly wasn't a highlight of my life, but I couldn't let it become anything more than a disgusting inconvenience.

Not long after that incident on the bus, I would face my biggest test as a man. A test that would have been difficult to pass without my faith. And my faith at this point in my life and career wasn't where it should have been. I wasn't reading my Bible consistently, studying the Word, or praying nearly enough. I wasn't living my life for Christ. I was making compromises, and I found myself facing the consequences of one of them that spring.

My play that season in Springfield mirrored what was going on in the rest of my life. On the field, I was up and down. Looking like a future major leaguer in one game, then a Single-A scrub in the next. As further evidence of my inconsistency, I eventually led the entire league in both hit batters and strikeouts, and I was right up there in total walks as well. There were times I felt lost, while at other times I was dominant, confident, and sharp. Off the field, Jenn and I were having ups and downs ourselves, and we faced something in our relationship that put us at a crossroads. She was in Springfield visiting me for a weekend that spring. We were eating at our favorite breakfast spot, and I could tell she was dealing with something intense. Couples certainly know the telltale signs that indicate something is wrong. Even though few words were being said, it was clear something was up.

"What's wrong?" I asked Jenn three times, and each time she refused to answer. She was uncharacteristically quiet. I had never seen her look so sad. I analyzed the look one more time, thought back on what had transpired with us the past few months, and a light went on: "You're pregnant." I went to her side of the table, pulled her in close to me, and said, "We'll be okay."

But truth be told, I was worried. The facts didn't look good. I could not afford to support a child. I had almost no money in my bank account and could barely live off what I was making. I found out later Jenn had been worried about my reaction. She also knew there would be some social judgment because we were people of faith but unmarried. She was fearful that if I acted excited, I would be faking it. She knows me well enough now to realize I'm not that good of an actor.

"Do you want me to quit baseball?" I asked her. "I'm not making any money right now. I can get some sort of job to support our family," I said, and I meant it too. That was probably the most logical scenario.

"No," Jenn said. "Don't do that. You don't have to do that. I don't want you feeling you have to stay with me because of the baby."

"Jenn, I'm with you for a reason," I told her. "I'm not dating you for a dead end. We're together for a reason." Hearing that from me definitely helped Jenn feel more secure about us, because at that point in our relationship, I had still not told her I loved her. It would be another full year before I would do that for the first time. Those words held such sacred meaning to me, I was adamant about not saying them until I was 100 percent certain I was speaking to the person I would be with forever.

What I learned later, and probably should have known then, is that women need to hear those words. I do realize that, and even though my intentions were good, I know that it was difficult for her to not have the reassurance of hearing me tell her I loved her when times were tough. I look back with some feelings of guilt that even in that moment, the most important of our time together, I still didn't say it to her.

It was reassuring to hear she didn't want me to quit baseball, even though I think I would have. Baseball was the only job I'd had or wanted, but at that point I had no money, and a baby on the way. The fact that she did not hesitate in telling me not to give up baseball is the reason I am still playing now. The upcoming months would be a trying time for Jenn and me, dealing with the distance between us both literally and figuratively. She was pregnant and back in Florida during that season, while I was riding buses across Missouri, Texas, Arkansas, and Oklahoma. We argued a lot, and there was tension between us that we had never felt before. I was feeling guilty and afraid, and I really didn't know what to do. Here I was, supposedly a Christian man, unmarried, and now preparing to have a child out of wedlock.

On top of that, I dreaded the thought of having to tell my family. I had no reason to believe they would be anything but supportive, but I couldn't shake the feeling that I had let so many people down. No matter how scared I was, this was the new reality in my life. We were having a baby, and I needed to inform my parents before they found out another way. My dad happened to have a trip planned to visit me in Springfield a few weeks after Jenn told me she was pregnant, so the timing was perfect for me to break the news to him. The problem was, I couldn't muster up the courage to do it the first two nights. On the final night after our game, we had dinner, but I still didn't break the news. My dad said he was going to stay out a little longer to watch the Cardinals play on TV before turning in and heading back to California in the morning. I headed back to my apartment but felt guilty. That's when I decided to call my dad.

"Dad, Jenn and I are having a baby. You're going to be a grandpa." I waited for the news to hit him, expecting to receive a humbling talk about being more responsible, but my dad ended up humbling me in a different way.

"Congratulations, son! We'll be here for you," he told me, excited for us and completely calming my fears that he might not understand. I called my mom to tell her the news as well and she was as equally excited. And while I had the weight of the world off my shoulders knowing my family was in my corner, I still had to figure out how I was going to take care of a baby. Jenn and I were at one of those pivotal points in a relationship where things could go in one of two different directions, and our lives would be defined forever by how we handled this. Either we were going to be galvanized by our circumstances and be together forever, or it could be over between us.

In addition to the upheaval in my personal life, I still had a job to do, and I needed to have a clear head in order to do it well. Here I was, about to become a father, living in a town I barely knew far from everyone I loved, broke, and trying to survive while living well below the poverty line. I was already motivated to make it to the major leagues as fast I could, but the reality of where my life was made it extra clear that I truly had no Plan B. There were now two additional people counting on me to step up and be the man I needed to be. I still had a long way to go.

CHAPTER 5

MARCH TO THE MAJORS

The summer I spent in Springfield in 2016 felt heavy. Emotionally, I was all over the map. Nervous and scared about the pending arrival of a baby, yet also excited about being a dad. Looking back, I'm sure I was suffering from some level of depression, being so far from Jenn and my family, completely broke and apprehensive about my future. I had a feeling of emptiness that seemed to hang over me like a cloud.

There were only eight teams in the entire league, so it seemed we were taking monotonous bus rides to the same locations and seeing the same players again and again. The only time I felt I had any control was when I was on the pitching mound every five days or so. Things weren't ideal in my personal life, so I tried to focus as much as I could on my job that season. I wanted to be as dominant as possible and hopefully stand out. A promotion to Triple-A could solve a lot of problems.

I made the midseason all-star team that played in our home ballpark, and was one of the best pitchers in the league, but I had the worst ERA of my career. I was constantly reminded how my pitching performance mirrored the personal life I had little control over. The bursts of anger I'd experienced as a young kid would emerge now and then on the dusty fields we played on in Arkansas, Texas, Oklahoma, and Missouri. We faced the Dodgers affiliate from Tulsa on our home field one day, and I was cruising along with a shutout in the seventh inning. I was throwing a gem, which wasn't an easy task considering future National League MVP Cody Bellinger was on that Tulsa team, as dangerous at the plate then as he is now, terrorizing major-league pitchers. There was a runner on first with two outs, and I faced a batter with a 3-2 count. I was seconds away from shutting out my opponent for a full seven innings when the manager walked to the mound to give me the hook. As he walked to the mound, I shook my head in frustration. "Really?" I said to him as he took the ball out of my hand.

"If you have a problem with that, then go talk to Gary," he yelled back at me as I exited the field. He meant Gary LaRocque, the Cardinals director of player development. That last pitch was my one hundredth of the game, but I wasn't under a pitch count, so it infuriated me to be pulled this close to seven shut-out innings, with a 3-2 count and two outs no less. If the next pitcher came into the game and allowed the runner on base to score, that would count against me. I didn't want anything impeding my advancement to Triple-A, and I felt I had enough strength to get out of the inning. My teammate and friend came in and struck the last guy out, but, nonetheless, the friction continued on the bench. My pitching coach took his turn chewing me out. "If you want to stay in the game longer, then throw more strikes," he said. A few days later, I was throwing in the bullpen when the pitching coach got on me again. "Someone with a background like you who went to four different colleges? It just shows that you can't fit in," he said.

"You have no idea what my story is!" I snapped back. "I had my scholarship pulled from one school and then I had my eligibility taken away. That's why I had to keep transferring." He assumed I was a problem child who needed to keep transferring because nobody wanted him in their program. Getting into a shouting match with a coach wasn't the right thing for me to do, but I felt I had to let him know the truth. I had to defend myself. I've taken intense criticism throughout my career in all three sports, but that was the final straw. Looking back, all of those outbursts that season probably manifested from the personal issues I was experiencing. The short fuse was connected to my guilt.

While I was wrapping up that season of Double-A ball, Jenn was back in Florida preparing to be a mom, stocking up on things we would need to bring a baby into the world, like a stroller, crib, high chair, and other things I had no clue about. I was no help to her at all. You'd think I was an alien dropped onto earth, completely intimidated by a Babies R Us store. Diaper Genie? Is that something you rub to have a genie pop out to change a dirty diaper? Let's get one of those. We did know we were having a boy, and we celebrated the news with a gender reveal party in Springfield when Jenn came to town along with her parents, grandparents, sister, and best friend.

Everything going on that summer provided me a much needed wake-up call. I needed to clean up and tighten every aspect of my life. My physical and spiritual body had plenty of room for improvement. I decided that if there were aspects of my life I could upgrade, I was going to try. The starting point was my relationship with the Lord. It wasn't anywhere close to being where it should be. I made a conscious effort to spend more time reading the Bible in those months. I had my laptop computer with me and I used it to watch little documentary

Bible stories for hours each week. I also tried to eat more healthily, making better choices for meals. I started taking probiotics, and even though it was difficult with limited options and a scarcity of funds, I tried to select foods that were less processed and not fried.

When the season ended, I packed my truck and returned to Florida, knowing the next time I wore a baseball uniform I would be a father. As for being a husband, Jenn and I did not feel this was the time to get married. Financially, it was impossible. Thankfully, we had support from Jenn's family, and that off-season her grandpa gave me a job with his company again. Emotionally, I was unable to provide what Jenn would need from me as a husband. I just didn't have it in me at this point in my life, and I was adamant about not trying to act like I did. While Jenn and I weren't arguing constantly, our relationship wasn't set upon the foundation it needed to thrive as a married couple. I was truly fearful of setting myself up for divorce by rushing into a marriage that we weren't prepared for. I still couldn't tell Jenn I loved her at this point, as I wasn't sure when we would get married. I can only imagine the insecurity that created within Jenn to not have me tell her, but I worried that saying it could mislead her into thinking we'd get married. The life-changing event of having a baby was enough to occupy us both, and his arrival was rapidly approaching.

Jenn's due date was November 20, 2016. We visited the doctor a few days prior to see if she was dilated and were told she wasn't, so the doctors sent us home with a couple of old wives' tales containing ideas to jump-start the labor process. One trick Jenn tried was eating macaroni and cheese smothered in barbecue sauce. Jenn actually loved it, and she still eats it that way now. She devoured as much spicy food as possible, thinking that would help. We bought a yoga exercise ball and Jenn bounced on that. I took her to the gym with me, and she spent some time on the treadmill. I'm not sure which, if any, method worked, but on November 24 we welcomed our son, Casen, to the world.

I'm guessing a lot of first-time dads can relate to my experiences at the hospital the day Casen was born. If you asked Jenn to describe the situation, she might tell you she was dealing with two babies that day. One had a great excuse, considering he was just born. The other was me, and I know my downfall was mistakenly taking a peek behind the curtain in the middle of all the action. I nearly passed out. I wasn't prepared for what bombarded my senses. I had planned on cutting the umbilical cord like most proud dads, but that plan was scrapped when I got light-headed, pale, and sick to my stomach. Jenn also said I was making gurgling sounds as I nearly passed out. Meanwhile, as I was trying to regain my senses, I could see the doctor tapping Casen with a mallet. I later learned that it is standard in a delivery room, but at the time, it just added to my disorientation and self-induced panic.

We all survived that day just fine, even me, and while Jenn was instantaneously natural and amazing as a mom, I tried my best to help as much as my limitations would allow. Baseball players who are multiskilled are called "five-tool players." The five tools are speed, power, the ability to hit for average, arm strength, and great defensive ability. When it came to my abilities as a new dad, I would call myself a four-tool player. I could hold, rock, feed, and change wet diapers. No problem. Messy diapers were my downfall. They were out of my comfort zone and ability, so I avoided them like a vegan avoids a meat lover's pizza.

I had a couple of months to be around Jenn and Casen before the start of spring training in 2017—what I considered to be the most critical point of my career. I couldn't fathom going back to Springfield for another season of Double-A ball, though it was a possibility. I was motivated to be promoted to the Triple-A team in Memphis for a number of reasons, one being the pay raise that went with it. My salary would increase to $2,100 per month. In addition, if I were called up to the major league team at any point, even for just a single game or a weekend series, I would be paid $3,000 per day, and be placed on what's called the 40-man roster. That would automatically increase my salary to $88,000 for the remainder of that season, even if I was sent back to Memphis. For the first time, I had a chance to earn a livable wage by playing baseball.

There was a lot at stake and the next few weeks in spring training would be critical. Things were good with Jenn as I left for Jupiter, though marriage was still not something that was on my mind. I needed to get my career on track...now. I knew anything was possible in the 2017 season, including pitching for the Cardinals. I wanted to start fast and stand out, and physically I felt strong at 205 pounds.

Spring training went well. In my first Grapefruit League appearance, we faced the Boston Red Sox. Pablo Sandoval, a former World Series hero for the San Francisco Giants, hit a fastball I floated over the plate right up the middle. It took one hop and drilled me in the left butt cheek. I turned my body just in time and it didn't even hurt. Mike Matheny, the manager of the Cardinals, came out to check on me.

"How you feeling? You okay?" he asked.

"I'm fine," I told him as I lobbied to stay in the game.

He took me out as a precaution, so I went to the clubhouse, took a shower, and headed home. There was no reason for me to give that incident any more thought. I didn't reflect back and think what would have happened if the ball had traveled a couple of inches in a different direction. Or if I had turned too late. When you are a pitcher, you realize things like that are possible, and luckily for me, at that point in my career, it was one of the few times I had experienced being hit by a batted ball.

As spring training wound down, I had no idea where I would be assigned to start the season. I knew where I wanted to go: Memphis. I felt I'd pitched well enough to start the season in Triple-A. I had proven myself in the lower levels the past few seasons, and being told anything else was going to be a huge shock, and an even bigger disappointment. I received my marching orders just days before we broke camp.

"Daniel, we're sending you to Springfield. We're going to use a six-man rotation there," the pitching coordinator informed me. My heart stopped. I could feel the blood rush from my face. I had been expecting him to tell me I would start the season in Memphis.

"Why?" I asked, but I knew an explanation wouldn't make me feel any better, and it wouldn't have made a difference. It was the decision of the organization, and I had no choice but to live with it.

I was numb. More than that, I was ticked off. I had spent the previous season proving I didn't belong in Double-A anymore. I threw 150 innings that season and made the all-star team.

I felt that I had checked all the boxes and done everything I needed to do to move up to Triple-A. There was nothing left for me to prove in Springfield. Making matters even worse, they later told me I was actually going to be part of a five-man rotation that used six pitchers. That meant I wasn't included in the regular rotation and would start games only on occasion.

It was another low point in my career. Not only did I have my heart set on playing in Memphis, but there was no doubt in my mind I'd earned the opportunity to be there. I felt that was where I belonged. Yet here I was, yet again, packing my truck and heading to some place I didn't want to be. It was a professional setback, no question about it, and it would prove to be even more devastating personally. I tried to process what this would mean to my relationship with Jenn. I'd be back to making minimum wage, taking fifteen-hour bus rides, and living eleven hundred miles away from my newborn son and girlfriend. If Jenn began to look at things objectively, she might not view me as marriage material.

I arrived in Springfield. Our season started in suburban Dallas—Frisco, Texas. I was still internally fuming as the series began, so I called Tim Leveque, the Cardinals' minor league pitching coordinator, to try to get some clarity of why I was here.

"What is going on, Tim?" I asked. "I'm the only returning starter in Springfield, and I don't even get a normal spot in the rotation?"

He explained that it was just the way things had worked out. There was nothing that I could have done. What happened next was almost a replay of the season before. Two days later, as I was walking into the weight room for a pregame workout, and before I had even thrown a single pitch in a game that season, I received a call from Gary LaRocque. He had good news. He told me to pack up—I was going to Memphis. What was funny about that call was that early in the conversation, Gary scolded me for not reaching out to him instead of Tim when I was asking about why I was still in Double-A. Then he gave me the life-changing news. I was going to be in Triple-A, one injured or slumping Cardinals pitcher away from being called up to the big leagues. I was so excited as I hastily made arrangements to get to Tennessee, I could have walked and been there on time.

• • •

By now it had been almost two weeks since I had last pitched a game, and that was in sunny Florida in March. The calendar had turned to April, and I was scheduled to start the home opener for the Memphis Redbirds against the Colorado Springs Sky Sox. I went through my normal routine preparing for that game, and I remember two things about the night. One, I was incredibly happy. Everything in my life felt different and better being at this level. The Redbirds stadium is located in downtown Memphis, so just being in that urban setting, surrounded by large buildings, gave everything a more big-time vibe. I felt I was in the big leagues already in some respects. Two, the other thing that stood out was my mind-set. I wanted to dominate, even at this higher level of competition. I had faced big league batters during spring training, so I knew I could hold my own. Double-A ball was in my rearview mirror. Even though I loved the charming city of Springfield, I was very much okay with not being there. I wanted to get this next phase of my career off to a good start, and with God helping me in that game, I did. We beat the Sky Sox 5–1. Josh Hader, now a major league all-star with the Milwaukee Brewers and one of the top closers in baseball, started for Colorado Springs. On that night, I out-dueled him. Another highlight of my first start happened after the game. My phone rang as I was getting ready to leave the clubhouse. It was Jenn.

"Hi," she said. "What are you doing?"

"Grabbing some food and heading home," I told her. "Take a look to your left," she instructed me. I turned and there she was. She had driven all the way to Memphis from North Carolina with her dad and Casen to watch my debut. That made the night even more special, and things continued to go well that entire first month.

The new scenery in Memphis made me feel so grateful. The pay bump was a welcome relief, and I enjoyed my teammates and coaches. It was a fantastic professional environment that I embraced immediately. Being in Triple-A meant the long bus rides were a thing of the past. A typical road trip in this league meant taking a bus from the stadium to the airport in Memphis and boarding a flight to a regional hub in a city like Denver, Charlotte, or Chicago. From there we would make a connection to Omaha, Des Moines, Colorado Springs, Oklahoma City, Albuquerque, or Fresno. The hotel accommodations on road trips in Triple-A were better also, as we normally stayed in a Hilton Garden Hotel or something similar, and we could choose our roommates. Better travel conditions. Roomier hotels. Improved ballparks and facilities. It all made a difference. Sometimes the psychological effects were as great as the actual physical and tangible upgrades. I just knew I was happy, pitching well, and in a good spot in my life and career.

On April 28, 2017, we hosted the Round Rock Express. I pitched a good game, and we won easily, 9–1. More significantly, it would be my last start in my new hometown that season, though I didn't know it at the time. I wouldn't be the winning pitcher in a game again until twelve months later. The one run I gave up in the sixth inning of the game that day stood out. I was standing on the mound when I thought I heard the PA announcer say the "pitcher" was coming to the plate. I may have subconsciously taken my foot off the gas a little bit, thinking I could get him out without my best pitch. He ended up blasting a cut fastball over the fence, ruining my shutout. I was annoyed at myself for tainting a good game by giving up a home run to a pitcher and having a mental lapse. It should never have happened. I returned to the dugout and said to a teammate, "I can't believe I let a pitcher get me."

"That wasn't a pitcher, Ponce," he told me. "That was a pinch hitter." I felt better knowing I'd just misunderstood the PA announcer. We then packed our bags for a road trip that took us to Omaha and Des Moines. I was 2-0 early in the season, feeling as confident and satisfied as I had been my entire career. We were heading out on the road for what was supposed to be a week. That road trip for me ended up lasting over a month.

During spring training, I had attended a regular Bible study group that included players from the Miami Marlins, Houston Astros, New York Mets, St. Louis Cardinals, and Washington Nationals. During one of our meetings, a pitcher for the Marlins named Adam Conley introduced our group to a prayer that really hit home for me. There are certain things that trigger something inside us, perk our ears up more and leave a lasting impression. That's what this particular prayer did for me. The words of Adam's prayer penetrated my soul at that moment, and they turned out to be prophetic: "Fill me with Your Holy Spirit; make me more like Christ; I am at Your disposal." I quickly memorized those words, and I was so moved by them that I vowed to recite this prayer every time I took the mound that season. I specifically remember Adam telling me to be careful when I said this prayer, because declaring that "I am at Your disposal" means the Lord can use you in any way He desires, and that you are surrendering your life for God to use in His ultimate wisdom. The words strengthened me for some reason. Having God use me the way He saw fit was appealing to me. I wanted that. I prayed that prayer before each start I made early in that 2017 season, and I repeated it often in between starts. My game-day routine when I was starting included doing my warm-up drills, throwing a pregame session in the bullpen, then returning to the dugout to wait for the start of the game. Finally, sitting on the bench before the first pitch, I would say that prayer: "Fill me with Your Holy Spirit; make me more like Christ; I am at Your disposal." On a warm spring day just weeks after hearing those words for the very first time, God heard them as well. And He decided to act on them.

CHAPTER 6

DEATH DENIED

D aniel is conscious, Ramon, but I need to let you know that the concern for the doctors is the bleeding going on in his skull. If that continues, they will need to operate, and they are going to have to get your authorization for it."

"Yes. I authorize you to do whatever you need to do immediately," my dad told the surgeon, still trying to process the emotions of what had suddenly occurred. My dad knew every second was critical. Immediately after giving the authorization, he dropped to his knees. He was in tears, praying. My mom was working, and my dad waited to tell her what had happened until he received more information, because he felt she would have been hysterical. My dad was truly shaken. As he packed his bags, he began to think more clearly. He began calling other family members, informing them of what happened and making one specific request of all of them: Pray.

Meanwhile, just minutes from the hospital where I was being prepped for surgery, the baseball game I had started had concluded. The team bus pulled up in front of the hospital, and Scott Ensell grabbed just his backpack from the bus, erroneously thinking that would be all he needed for a short stay in the hospital with me. He let his suitcase go back with the team to Memphis on the bus. In that backpack, Scott had just one other outfit packed to go along with his Memphis Redbirds windbreaker and a pair of dirty navy-blue pants. Instead of wearing that every single day for what would turn out to be the next twelve days, he purchased an Iowa Hawkeyes polo shirt that was on sale for a few dollars in the hospital gift shop. For the remainder of his stay, he was asked if he had gone to school there.

"Get up, Daniel! We need you to wake up!" was the first thing I remember hearing as I came out of surgery. The doctors who had just performed a miracle on the operating table were now asking me to do something I felt was impossible. Wake up. A few hours earlier, a portion of my skull had been sawed off and removed. Now here I was: groggy, in a fog, alive, and so tired that all I could think of doing was going back to sleep. I had no idea if it was day or night. By this time, my dad, along with Jenn and Casen, had joined Scott in the recovery room. A series of miraculous circumstances meant they were not making funeral arrangements. There's no way to overstate just how blessed I was to still be alive. If Scott had not made it to the mound as quickly as he did and had not been as decisive as he was, there would have been a different outcome. If the ambulance had not been immediately available, if the hospital had not been as close to the stadium as it was, and if the team of doctors that saved me had not been working that afternoon, my risk of death would have been much higher. It's hard to put into words how humbling it is to know your life was placed in the hands of other people, and their talent and their professionalism were the reasons you survived.

The doctor's official diagnosis of my injury read this way: *Markedly abnormal. Comminuted, depressed fracture of the right anterior (squamosal) temporal bone with a large epidural hematoma (traumatic accumulation of blood between the skull and the dural membrane).* More simply stated, I had a large epidural hematoma and skull fracture. Even more simple than that: The injury to my skull was akin to a shattered windshield. I had suffered a primary skull fracture, but there were also cracks spreading from the site because of the impact of the baseball hitting me. The hematoma was what turned it into a life-and-death situation.

As it was explained to me later, the surgery entailed cutting away a piece of my skull to relieve the pressure on my brain and stop or at least slow the bleeding inside. The procedure took several hours, and Scott was there the entire time, processing information he received from hospital staff and sharing it with Jenn and my dad as they made their way to Iowa, as well as with the Cardinals organization. When the surgery was over, Scott relayed the news from the neurosurgeon that things had gone as well as they could possibly hope for with such an invasive and severe procedure. They placed a draining tube in my head, and then reaffixed the portion of my skull that had been removed. Scott told us the tube looked like a turkey baster. Essentially, it was a hand pump on a blood pressure cuff that sat in a shirt pocket of my hospital gown.

I was in the intensive care unit for over a week. Scott learned that the nurses would drain that pump frequently. In fact, on the first night immediately following the operation, they emptied a lot of blood. Scott would later share other discussions he'd had with the doctors during the surgery. He said that they placed a device in my head that was monitoring the pressure, which was essential to understanding my prognosis. If the emergency brain surgery was successful, then the pressure readings would stay down, and I would recover. If the bleeding intensified, then the pressure readings would go up, and I would require a second surgery. *Nobody* wanted a second surgery. The doctors would not be able to replace the piece of bone they cut away; instead, a wire mesh would be inserted into my skull, likely leading to a long-term disability. A second surgery would increase all of the associated risks, so Scott was glued to the pressure monitor for the rest of the operation and throughout the night, watching it like a money manager obsessively monitors the stock market during a crash. The doctors had decoded the readings for him, so he followed them in real time, knowing the razor-thin margin for error. "I was praying nonstop for those numbers to not increase," Scott told Jenn and my dad after they arrived. "A few times they got to within a tenth of a point of the maximum threshold." He was exhausted from watching that monitor, willing the numbers to not rise even a fraction higher. The decisions made before and during the operation were swift, and most of them carried huge implications.

One clear memory I have after regaining consciousness is seeing my dad in the room, and he gave me details of the surgery and everything I had gone through. He had to, because I had no idea what had transpired.

"Wait. When did I have surgery?" I asked.

I could still vividly see the pitch I threw across the plate that in a split second was on a high-velocity collision course with my head. A part of me continued to believe that I had suffered only a concussion. I tried to figure out why I was in a hospital room. I really wasn't interested in hearing too many details, though, because all I wanted to do was sleep. Talking hurt my head. I asked my dad to pray for me, and he did. My dad put the Lord first in his life, and I knew the words he spoke would be as powerful as any I could hear. Because of my dad's deep faith, God has placed a calming spirit on his soul that allows him to be stoic and under control in the midst of extreme crisis. He needed to rely on all of his faith in this moment, as he willed himself to believe things would be okay. He prayed over me with the words from Romans 8:28: "*And we know that in all things God works for the good of those who love him, who have been called according to his purpose.*" My dad made it clear that he believed the Lord was going to be working in this situation and that there was a reason for it. The strength and optimism he was able to receive and convey to everyone for the next few weeks came from believing the Lord would both heal me and work through me and this injury.

Jenn later told me that when she arrived in Iowa and saw me

for the first time after surgery, it was worse than she'd expected. She described me as looking like a zombie, with tubes coming out of my half-shaved head. She said she could see the incision and dried blood around it.

When I think back to the time after surgery, it's incredible to consider the difference between where my life started that day and where it was twelve hours later. In the early afternoon, I was making my sixty-second professional start on a glorious afternoon in a stadium packed with people. My agent, Brian, believed I was on the cusp of being called up to the major leagues, thinking it could happen within days. He felt I was next in line to be promoted when the team needed pitching help. Now I was lying on a hospital bed in the ICU, with my skull reassembled and a hospital chaplain waiting nearby just in case things took a turn for the worse. Which was still very possible. Playing baseball again seemed completely out of the question, and the immediate goal for the doctors was simply to enable me to live a life remotely similar to the one I had known.

Scott, Jenn, and my dad all told me that internally, they were bracing for the harsh reality that I would live with some sort of cognitive disability. The blow could have affected my senses, and it certainly could have destroyed my memory and ability to process simple information.

But the combination of faith, prayers, and an incredible medical team prevented the worst-case scenario from occurring. And ever so slowly, I inched along a very methodical road to recovery. In those early days after surgery, I sensed that everyone around me was treating me delicately, for obvious reasons.

My agent spent a lot of time in those early days talking to Jenn and my dad on the phone, discussing the prospects of my being able to lead a normal life. Functioning as a normal person in society was the number one goal. In those early days, my short-term and long-term health were the only things discussed.

I spent three and a half weeks in Iowa, including a full week in intensive care. I slowly began to do more, and I was allowed to initiate more movement. Sitting up in my bed was an early milestone. Taking a few slow steps, and then progressing to longer walks in the hallways, was a big deal. Though I was losing weight very rapidly, and eventually dropped a total of eighteen pounds, I felt my body was intact and functioning. Everything felt normal to me except my head, and that's what concerned my family and the doctors, and kept their expectations of what kind of life I could look forward to grounded.

In addition to Jenn, her dad, Casen, my dad, and the nurses and support staff streaming in and out, eventually there would be something else that made its presence felt in the recovery room—an elephant. At some point, Jenn flat out asked the doctor the question we were all silently pondering: "Do you think Daniel will be able to play baseball again?"

The doctors subtly tried to change the subject and warned us to manage our expectations and keep things in perspective. "Let's focus first on getting Daniel to master some of the basic movements we need to see. Before we start thinking about baseball, we need to start with baby steps," they replied. While I was prepared to take those baby steps forward, I almost took one giant leap back. I was doing well enough after a week to be moved out of intensive care and into a more general area of the hospital. On the very first night, I didn't receive the sodium the doctors insisted I have. Although I was hooked up to numerous cords and wires, at one point I felt I needed to get up and go to the bathroom.

"What are you doing?" my dad yelled at me as I tried to disconnect everything connected to me. He noticed that something was off with me and called for the nurse to come in. That's when they realized I had missed the sodium, and I was placed back in intensive care. After discussing it with doctors, my dad figured out why it's imperative for people who are in my condition to have sodium. Simply put, it is critical in this early recovery period to retain water.

"Are you telling me that the water is retained in the body and pulled from the brain?" my dad asked a doctor when I was back in ICU.

"That's exactly right," the doctor replied.

"Amazing," my dad said. In order to keep water away from my brain, they would keep my sodium levels high, and the sodium would pull water from my brain and keep it dehydrated. Shortly after this mini-crisis was averted, I asked the doctor if I could start looking at screens to combat the boredom and monotony of being in a hospital. He allowed me to use my phone and iPad, so I was able to watch Cardinals games when they were on.

I was moved from the ICU again after my sodium levels were stable, and each day I felt I was getting a little better physically. I was still tired and wanted to sleep as much as possible, but my walks were getting longer, and I was a little less worn out from them each day. And while my head was nowhere near being healed, I was progressing. I was looking forward to leaving the hospital and being able to shower in my own bathroom. Alone. The few times I got frustrated in the hospital were when I couldn't do menial things on my own. The only thing I was cleared to do by myself was use the bathroom. Other than that, there was always someone around me. I was starting to get rail-thin, but I knew I would be able to put the lost weight back on quickly when I left the hospital.

One thing I had no shortage of in the hospital was time to think, and I used those moments to take inventory of where my faith was. Once my dad prayed over me following the surgery, I started praying as much as I could. I remember being so grateful that I was alive. I was constantly praying, thanking God, and I would often think back to the prayer I learned in the Bible study group in spring training. The prayer about God using me as a vessel in whatever way He wanted. I recall lying on my hospital bed and thinking, "What am I doing? Why wasn't I all in on my faith?" I had been spared, given another chance at life. I was ashamed of where my faith was. I knew I had to do better, and I vowed to take my faith to another level. Because of the length of my hospital stay, the seriousness of my injury, and the uncertainty of my prognosis, I could have easily spiraled into depression. I think God spared me from that too. I made a very conscious effort to keep my mind and thoughts on something bigger than myself. I warded off any feelings of self-pity. And I honestly never doubted I would play baseball again, so it's not like I felt my career was going to be cut short. I knew I was feeling better and stronger physically, with no lasting issues with anything but my head. Jenn was by my side every day, taking the day shift at the hospital, while my dad spent every night there. Dad set the tone for my recovery with his incessant positive attitude. He has a big personality, it's infectious, and some of his never-ending positivity seemed to rub off on everybody. My dad puts God at number one in his life, and his belief is that everything happens for a reason, even serious head injuries. He felt the Lord was going to do work through my injury. My dad doesn't panic during a crisis; in fact, he's more confident and calm when things are chaotic. He felt he had a job to do, and that was making sure the hospital staff was operating on all cylinders and doing everything possible to make sure I would be okay. He was constantly getting information, asking questions, and sharing what he learned. I was very lucky to have Jenn and my dad supplying constant support. There was always a family member by my side.

Scott stayed in the hospital with me almost two full weeks. He was selfless, putting his entire professional and personal life on hold, sporting that Iowa Hawkeyes polo shirt nearly every day. There's no way to overstate how much he did for me. On top of his responsiveness on the mound when I got hit, and making those immediate life-and-death decisions, he was facilitating efforts behind the scenes in a way that wound up saving me financially. The costs of my medical care were going to be astronomical. Additionally, there were the added costs of hotel rooms, food, travel, and living expenses. Scott was in touch with the Cardinals, specifically the general manager at the time, John Mozeliak, who eventually told my dad that the club would take care of every single expense we incurred, including the ambulance ride, surgery, hospital stay, therapy, medications, hotel bills, food, plane flights, and any other associated costs.

"Don't worry about anything; we've got it covered," John told my dad. "Once you get all the receipts, just send them to my secretary and we'll get everything squared away. Don't even think twice," he said. It was an incredible gesture by a franchise known to be as classy as any in professional sports. I tried to make a point of expressing my gratitude for what the club did for me in almost every interview going forward. I wanted to express my appreciation publicly for the way the team had looked after me.

At this point, all the evidence pointed toward my not playing baseball again. I'm not sure what the Cardinals as an organization thought at the time. But I'm quite sure they weren't penciling me into any future lineups. What's funny is that I had the opposite belief. Even when things were at their worst, I never once doubted that my brain and head would eventually heal, and I would be back. Nothing had happened to my arm. Or my core. My legs were eventually going to be strong enough to drive off the mound. I knew it would take time, but I knew that day would come.

After twenty-five days, I was able to walk out of the hospital and into a hotel in Des Moines. Just that move alone allowed me to experience a little normalcy. I could now shower on my own. (If you don't think that is something to be grateful for, invite an audience for every shower you take for three straight weeks.) Jenn, Casen, and I could walk outside and go to eat at a restaurant. Two days later the doctors cleared me to fly, and Jenn booked flights for the three of us to head back to Florida. It was the most logical place for me to continue my rehab, since Jenn lived there and the Cardinals facility in Jupiter was close to Jenn's home. Furthermore, there was a renowned rehabilitation clinic in Daytona Beach, a short drive from Jenn's house.

Jenn was with me every single day, caring for me, encouraging me, while also taking care of Casen, who was still nursing. She was juggling so much and dropped everything in her life to be next to me. While I was in the hospital, she would often tell me she loved me. I was practically on my deathbed, and you'd think finally saying those three words would be the easiest thing I could have done during my entire stay in the hospital, yet I stubbornly refused to do so because I still wasn't ready to get married. I never told Jenn that I loved her back. Not once. I knew it bothered her. I didn't doubt she would be the woman I would eventually marry; I just wasn't in a position where I could take such a big step. Yet.

With a return to baseball at the forefront of my mind, I continued to get stronger every day. I was medically cleared to start doing baseball rehab exactly three months after the injury. I would put myself in position to test my arm and see if there was any residual damage. I threw a tennis ball to my dog Molly in the middle of the street when I was walking her. I had to see what I was capable of, and I admit, I made Molly run half a block or so chasing that ball sometimes. The next step for me was to regain the weight I had lost. I became almost obsessed researching healthy diets on Google, and I was especially focused on furthering my knowledge of probiotics and learning as much as I could about superfoods.

As great and supportive as the Cardinals organization had been, I don't think they were expecting me to come back. I didn't blame them. I imagined that no MLB team had ever dealt with such a situation. There was no handbook for a pitcher returning from a near-fatal brain injury. The team, focused on my health and well-being, was hopeful that I would be back to doing normal, everyday things. I had to assume they weren't looking at me as a legitimate potential starting pitcher at Busch Stadium.

I would get my chance to show the progress I had made, and at the same time convince the team that I should still be part of their plans. There was a business decision the Cardinals had to make regarding me. The 2017 season was my first "protection year," which meant the club had to decide if it was going to add me to its 40-man roster in the off-season or keep me on the Triple-A roster. This was something my agent, Brian, and I discussed while I was working my way back into shape. For weeks I had been lifting weights, running, stretching, eating properly, and doing everything I could off the field to make I sure I could get back on it. The Cardinals did not protect me, which meant I would have the chance to be selected by any other team in the Rule 5 draft (kind of a supplemental draft for players with a certain number of years in the minor leagues) in December. At some point, I had to get on the mound and show the Cardinals, and twenty-nine other teams, I could still be a top pitching prospect. It was September 2017, four months post-surgery, and I was ready to go full speed. With the thought of my future constantly on my mind, I had to prove that I was good to go. For four straight months, I drove to Palm Beach for a weeklong "Performance Camp." The camp, intended for the youngest players in the organization, was where the team introduced weight lifting and other training techniques. I was the oldest dude there by far. I was twenty-six, while most of the other players were seven or eight years younger. In fact, my roommate was an eighteen-year-old. I was named the "champ of the camp," since I had played four years of college and pitched hundreds of innings in the minors while most of these kids had recently attended their senior prom.

My arm felt great because I had barely pitched that season. Yes, I was coming off a catastrophic head injury, but my arm was as strong and fresh as ever. I felt there was finally a chance to change the narrative. I didn't want every thought and every story written about me to be a recounting of the injury I'd incurred in Iowa. The only way to make sure of that was by facing professional players in live batting practice at the Cardinals facility in Jupiter. It was September 29. With my future as a professional athlete on the line, I walked to the mound for the first time in four months and faced the Cardinals prospects who were preparing to play in the Arizona Fall League.

"I don't need that. You can slide it off the field," I said as the protective L-screen was being dragged toward the pitching mound. I didn't want to do this live batting practice session with training wheels. The L-screen would protect me from line drives a batter sent screaming at me. But I wouldn't have the option of using one during a game when I came back, so I certainly didn't want one now. I could sense that the young minor leaguers assigned to hit against me that day were a little tentative. A little timid in their swings because they knew of my history.

"Don't act like you can hurt me, guys. Swing those bats. You aren't going to hurt me," I barked at them authoritatively from the mound. It felt good to have my adrenaline flowing again, to feel the charge of having to perform. The session went well. I didn't feel like I had anything to prove to myself. I knew I could do this. I was here to show the Cardinals, and any other team, that my fastball was still alive. The session went well. Afterward, I felt I had checked a box and accomplished what I needed to do. I was a baseball player again, and not just someone who had been seriously injured playing baseball.

With my professional life arcing in the right direction, I got to work trying to fix things in my personal life. The most intense and emotionally challenging thing I had to do during the fall of 2017 was attend relationship therapy classes with Jenn. She had to be completely fed up with my nonsense about not being ready to say "I love you" or to get married. I couldn't blame her for wondering if I would ever be ready to step up and be a husband and a father. She knew that the guilt of having a baby and living together when we weren't married was eating at me. I was feeling determined to make things right, and that included this intense counseling. I had to focus on doing not what I thought was right in my mind, but what was biblically right. Jenn was feeling guilty about having a baby outside of marriage, too, and we knew our relationship was suffering because of it. In those final two months of the off-season, we met with a church counselor every week. There were deep and personal issues that had not come to the surface with us, but they did in very powerful ways at these sessions. It was time for me to make a decision. Did I want to be married to this incredible woman and be the faith-filled, biblically anchored father of my child? Or would I just call it quits and be only a biological father, while someone else would act as Casen's dad when Jenn moved on? Jenn describes the commitment to counseling as something that really opened my eyes. I knew she was appreciative that I was not stubborn enough to refuse to go. We both knew that we were at a point where we had to do something or we were essentially done. The counselor addressed the urgency and laid out three options to us, and she was very blunt. Option one, she explained, was to continue to do what we were doing and live in sin. Option two was to find a way to co-parent from a distance but live separately. And option three was to do the right thing: get married and grow our family in God's love and grace.

At this point, I still had not told Jenn I loved her, and the counselor found that extremely odd. In fact, I think she found it odd that I didn't realize it was odd. "You need to tell her that," she implored me. "You need to say those words to her, Daniel. A woman needs to hear those words. If you really feel that way, you have to tell her."

"She will know when I'm ready," I stubbornly responded.

"No. You need to tell her now. Right here in this room," she corrected me. Finally getting the point, I immediately turned to Jenn, and I spoke the words she needed to hear and I needed to say: "I love you, Jenn."

CHAPTER 7

READY FOR A BREAKOUT

Jen and I soon took it a step further; we decided that it was time to get married and become a family. We both knew we had to stop living in sin, but we faced a challenge: spring training was set to begin in a matter of days. There was no time to plan the elaborate wedding that girls dream about when they are young. I'm sure Jenn would have loved to do something special, but it wasn't an option. We had to quickly plan a wedding and make this union official. The pastor at the church where we attended counseling was a big Cardinals fan, and he loved Jenn and me. He agreed to perform the ceremony. We kept it simple. We gathered Jenn's family, and a few friends at the back of the church. The pastor married us right there. I knew this was what I wanted, and everything changed instantly when we became husband and wife. I began telling Jenn I loved her all the time, and the pressure and guilt of not living our life according to God's plan went away.

The preceding year had been the most eventful of my life, and the start of spring training provided the backdrop for another bit of news and blessing from God: our brand-new official family was going to welcome a new addition.

It sounds trivial or cliché to say it's possible for faith to overcome fate. Can it really? Is it truly possible to trust God and His plan so much that the laws of logic and nature don't seem to apply? Could one line drive collide with a human skull and result in that person's being gifted with a new and more meaningful and impactful life? When I reported to spring training in 2018, these were the questions I was considering.

I was very motivated to prove I could still be a big league pitcher, especially since the minor league teams didn't seem so sure. A number of teams reached out to my agent for more details about my head injury before the Rule 5 draft, and a couple of clubs expressed interest in selecting me, but ultimately, I went unclaimed. I felt a bit let down, but I didn't blame the teams for having doubts and not feeling I was worth the risk.

The last thing I expected was an easy path back. So, with the realization that this could potentially be my final spring training ever, I went into camp laser-focused.

God provided me a great test right off the bat, as we faced the World Series champion Houston Astros in my first appearance on the mound that spring. Their leadoff hitter was all-star Alex Bregman. In four months, he would be named the MVP of the 2018 All-Star Game, but in this at bat in Florida, I struck him out. It was the first competitive situation I'd been in since being injured by the pitch in Iowa. The Cardinals training staff had provided me with a carbon fiber insert I wore inside my cap that was designed to protect pitchers from comebackers up the middle. That was the only change in my uniform, gear, or approach since before the injury. The biggest difference now from spring training the previous season, when I was an anonymous minor leaguer, was that my injury had become a popular topic with the media. I was asked a lot of questions about it, and my response was almost always the same. I would tell the beat writers and reporters, "Look, if you are going to judge me this season, judge me on how I play. Don't use the injury as the premise of every story." My injury was a nonissue to me. I felt completely normal. I was recovered.

Unfortunately, that strikeout of Bregman in my first

Grapefruit League game was one of the few highlights for me during a spring training that I would describe as average. And average doesn't get you into the major leagues. There weren't many things I did, good or bad, that moved the needle, so I started the 2018 season in the same spot where I'd ended in 2017. I went to Memphis with one goal: to be the best pitcher in Triple-A. I felt the Cardinals would need pitching help at some point in the 2018 season, and if I could be the best pitcher in Triple-A, I could help make the decision to call me up an easy one. I was both motivated and grateful and ready to be known as just a baseball player again.

The Memphis Redbirds schedule looks pretty similar each season, and sometime in April or May, we would make a trip west to Iowa to face the Cubs again. That trip was looming on the horizon in the spring of 2018. Others kept talking about the return to the scene of my injury, but I didn't think about it, place any significance on it, or even know exactly when it was coming up. The memory I have of facing the Iowa Cubs in 2018 had nothing to do with being on the road back in Des Moines. The memory is actually from a home game we played against the Cubs on April 14. I struck out twelve batters—that was, and still is, my personal record in a professional game. It was after that home stand that we set out for our back-to-back stops in

Omaha and Des Moines. The reporters were ready to play up the story line of my return to the scene of the injury, but I gave them nothing to work with. No juicy sentimental sound bites. No reflection on what it meant being back.

"I just want this to be old news," I told the *Des Moines Register* before a game. "It's no more. It doesn't affect me. I'm the same person I was before." I didn't want to make those games in Iowa about me, and, truthfully, I didn't even want to be there. I'm not sure if our manager, Stubby Clapp, set up our pitching rotation intentionally so I wouldn't be in line to make a start in Iowa, but I know that I sat on my butt in the dugout watching those three games. I didn't play. Not only that, I didn't look for the ambulance parked along the first-base side of the field and wonder if that was the one I rode in the previous year. I didn't envision our trainer, Scott, running to check on me as I slumped to the ground, or visit Mercy Medical Center to see if I could recognize any of the staff and say hi. The injury was in my past, and I saw no upside in rehashing anything about it.

That's not to say I didn't hold a very special place in my heart for Des Moines and Iowa Cubs fans. If I have any emotional trigger connected to my injury, it's because of what happened in the days and weeks and months that followed. The outpouring of support I received from fans in Des Moines was incredible. I still have the hundreds of cards and letters and handmade posters that people of all ages sent me. Other than that, the story was over in my mind. I had moved on in every conceivable way. (Maybe, someday, I'd write a book.) The 2018 season progressed, and by the end of May, my pitching performances were starting to convince people that my head injury in 2017 was nothing more than a footnote in my bio. Ancient history. That's what I hoped anyway.

I was consistent in those first two months. I had taught myself a new grip on my fastball and was happy with the results. I was getting batters to swing and miss more frequently, and, consequently, my strikeout rate went up.

As the calendar flipped from May to June and spring surged into the four-month sweatbox that is a Memphis summer, God continued to shine His grace on me...in a big way. Reno was in town for a three-game series that began on June 8. I had just pitched on the sixth of June against Tacoma, so my role for this series was to sit on the bench and cheer on my teammates. That's what I was doing when our pitching coach, Dernier Orozco, called me over and made an unusual request.

"Hey, Ponce, go inside and check the cameras," he told me. We have monitors in a little video room that showcase the feed from various cameras pointed on or near the field. These allow us to review our pitching form and pick up little tendencies that need to be corrected during the game or after it. It was a strange request, because never in my baseball life had I been told to do that while a game was in progress. I would have been less surprised if he had asked me to go to the clubhouse and bake him a cake. It felt odd, but I went inside to do as I was told.

"All the cameras look good," I informed him when I returned to the dugout.

"You sure?" he asked me, continuing on a subject I felt was dead.

"Yeah," I confirmed. Things got more bizarre as we were eating a postgame meal in the clubhouse. Our manager, Stubby Clapp, called me into his office, along with Orozco. I walked into an ambush. They scolded me about the videos again, implying I did something wrong. This strange day had now entered an alternate universe. I told them, again, that "yes, the cameras had all been working fine" when I inspected them.

"Well, we're going to look at some video now and check out your mechanics and see what's going on with you," they said.

We sat there a minute, then Stubby broke the silence. "Do you have any family in town, Ponce?" he asked me. I told him yes.

"Would they mind going to St. Louis and watching you pitch?"

Now things started making sense.

"No, they'd love doing that," I said as a smile broke across my face and my coaches burst out laughing.

"Well, good. You're going up to join the Cardinals tomorrow," my manager said.

I jumped up and hugged both guys. Stubby was recording the moment for me on his phone. When the euphoria subsided, reality set in. This was an exciting, exhilarating, powerful new sensation I had never experienced before. It had finally happened. I was on my way to St. Louis to make my Major League Baseball debut.

Jenn was waiting for me outside the clubhouse, as she normally was after a home game. I told her, "We're going to St. Louis." I could tell she was surprised, too, and trying to process the information. She was thrilled for me, excited for us, and a little overwhelmed, thinking of all we'd need to do to get on the road. I called my dad next, excited to share the news with the person who had waited to hear it as long as I had. All he did when I told him was scream at the top of his lungs. He was so loud that anyone near me could hear it blasting through my phone. Then he told my youngest sister and mom, who were nearby and wondering what the scream was for.

I called my agent next to share the news. The fact was this: The Cardinals were hosting the San Diego Padres and needed help in the bullpen for the three-game series. "Will I be starting one of the games?" I asked my manager, assuming he might have been told what I'd be doing.

"I'm not sure," he replied. If the plan was for me to make a start for the Cardinals, there was almost no way he wouldn't have been told, so I assumed I would be relieving. That would be something new. I had never done it before, but I certainly wasn't complaining. Jenn and I hustled home to start packing. My dad mobilized things on his end, informing my other two sisters and some of his friends of the big news, and they all made plans to travel to St. Louis on short notice to witness what we all thought would be the highlight of my career to this point.

As usual, God had a different plan for my debut in a major-league uniform. I remember how I felt when I found out I was being called up. I was thankful and grateful, but I was surprised that those emotions were coupled with a feeling of confusion. I kept asking myself "Why?" Why was God doing this? Why was He allowing this? The mixed emotions from the night before were still there the next morning as pregnant Jenn, Casen, and our dog Molly jumped in the car, and we departed from our apartment at around eight. Even on that drive, I couldn't shake the feeling of not knowing why this good thing was happening to me. "Why me?" I wondered. "Why now?"

When we arrived in St. Louis after the almost-five-hour drive, Jenn settled into the hotel while I went to the stadium to get ready for the game, still carrying the baggage of not quite believing I belonged or even deserved to be here. I changed into my Cardinals uniform and took in a sweeping panoramic view of the clubhouse. This locker room was nothing like the minor-league locker rooms I'd spent the past five years in. It was like comparing Disneyland to a roadside carnival.

By now I was in baseball mode, with those mixed messages that had been swirling in my mind long gone. We beat the Padres that night 5–2. The team didn't need me, and I never left the bullpen. It was the same story the next two nights. We lost both of those games by a score of 4–2. I had been called up, but never called on. I didn't throw a single pitch in those three games. I was technically now a major league player, but the one thing missing was the actual *playing* part of the equation.

After the final game of the series, I fully expected to be sent back down to Memphis, and I was surprised nobody approached me to immediately give me the news. Roughly thirty minutes after the game, I ran into our general manager, Mike Girsch.

"Have you talked to Matheny?" he asked me. I told him no, but shortly after, I did see our manager and he informed me I was going back to Memphis. He told me one thing that made me feel numb; he made a point to say that I was a big leaguer now. While that should have been the validation I needed to feel I deserved the promotion, I felt there had been situations where I could have been brought into the game. It made me angry that I was never given the chance. I went to dinner with Jenn, my dad, and my agent, Brian, and barely spoke. I was ticked off, and still simmering on the drive back. A lot of the anger stemmed from how all the close people in my life had dropped what they were doing to come see me play in St. Louis, but all they saw was a few games up close that I didn't play in. Those three days were like a blur. In some ways, it felt like it didn't even happen. We drove to St. Louis with me feeling that I didn't belong there, and we drove back to Memphis with me feeling that I had proven I was right.

As a Christian, I'd like to believe I always put my faith into action, so I put those thoughts aside. I snapped out of it, put a halt to the pity party, and shifted my thoughts to where they belonged. Up. To feeling thankful, grateful, and blessed beyond

Daniel with sisters Jackie, Bianca, and Julia (2000)

Daniel with sisters Jackie, Bianca, and Julia (2000)

Poncedeleon family (2002)

Poncedeleon family (2003)

With sister Julia (2004)

Pitching at La Mirada High School (2010)
(Courtesy of Carol Emerling)

Pitching at La Mirada High School (2010)
(Courtesy of Carol Emerling)

Dad with baby Casen (spring training 2017)

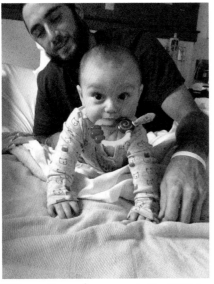

With son Casen after surgery in Des Moines, Iowa (2017)

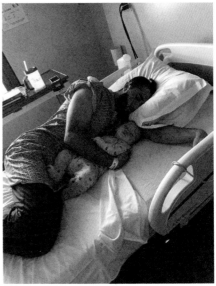

Napping with Casen post-surgery in Iowa (2017)

Hospital in Iowa with get well cards (2017)

With Casen in Florida after Iowa (2017)

Family in Florida after returning from Iowa (2017)

With family in California—Ramon, Casen, Daniel, Jenn, Bianca, Callum, Julia, Lilly, Jackie, Ollie, Charlotte, and Mary (2017)

With Dad, Ramon, at St. Louis BBWA
Awards dinner (2018)

Plaque from St. Louis BBWA Awards dinner (2018)

Family and friends at spring training (2018)

Ramon and Casen from spring training (2018)

Family at first MLB game (6/11/18)

Scoreboard during MLB debut (7/23/18)

Pitching at MLB debut (7/23/18)

Family after MLB debut (7/23/18)

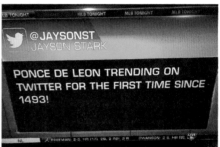

Jayson Stark's classic tweet during debut (7/23/18)

Family with MLB agent Brian Grieper after debut (7/23/18)

With Dad in spring training (2019)

Ponce de Leon family: Mila, Jenn, Casen, Daniel, and Molly
(Christmas 2019)

Ponce de Leon family: Casen, Daniel, Jenn, and Mila
(Christmas 2019)

Ponce de Leon family (2020)

belief to have earned enough trust with the Cardinals for them to bring me up as an insurance policy in the bullpen for a few days. The team's job was not to provide scenarios to make sure I lived out my dreams. I worked for the organization, and it was my role to help when and where I was needed. The fact was, the club didn't need me in those games. My best course of action would be to believe what my manager told me—that I actually *was* a big leaguer now—and then pitch well, be patient, and earn another chance to show everyone what I could do. I realized how shortsighted it was to be angry about not playing. Just being in that uniform had changed my life in a tangible way. By making that three-day trip to St. Louis, my pay increased. Instead of making $2,100 per month as a Triple-A player, I was now on the Cardinals 40-man roster. That was a huge deal. A minor league salary would be a thing of the past for me, and my salary was elevated to $88,000, which meant my take-home pay each month tripled. I also qualified for full health insurance coverage, an incredible blessing with a young child and a baby on the way.

I had experienced a whirlwind of emotions that had now come completely full circle. It started with gratitude when I received word of the promotion. That morphed into confusion, which was swept up into anger, then reverted back to gratitude.

A year before, I had just departed the hospital and faced an uncertain future in every aspect of my life. Now I was certain of one thing regarding my future: I'd get another chance to pitch for the Cardinals if I took care of business.

As a result of not pitching those days in St. Louis, and then waiting to get back into the rotation in Memphis, when I returned I was rusty. I felt out of sync on the mound and gave up eight runs in my first start. I never got back into the groove I felt I was in before my call-up in early June. July began with another trip to Des Moines, and this time I did make a start. I struck out eight Cubs on July 1, and I didn't give up an earned run. My goal was to win the game and make this trip to Des Moines even more anticlimactic than it was in April. Because it was our second visit there, the novelty of my return had subsided. I did face Victor Caratini again, and this time I struck out the batter who'd hit the line drive that struck me in 2017. I made a conscious effort to show my love and appreciation for as many Cubs fans as I could on that trip, but in every other regard, I treated it like it was just another game.

On July 6 and 15, I faced the Omaha Storm Chasers (the Triple-A team of the Royals), and I didn't allow an earned run in either game. I went the distance on the fifteenth, throwing a complete game shutout for the first time in my career. That would be my last start for Memphis until August. I was pitching as well as I had in my entire career. I had my groove back, and it earned me another promotion to St. Louis. This time there was much less pomp and circumstance attached to the news. No big reveal from my manager and pitching coach, no odd camera inspections. They just delivered the news.

The icing on the cake was learning I was scheduled to start a game for the Cardinals in Cincinnati, against the Reds, on July 23. The news was phenomenal on multiple levels. Starting allowed me to stay in my normal routine on days I wasn't pitching. It was what I was most comfortable doing. But there were some potential distractions I took precautions to avoid. One was managing the ticket requests for people who would want to make the trip to Ohio. I told everyone it was their choice: Come if you want to, but I completely understand if you can't. Jenn, Casen, and my dad would be there, of course, and knowing I was guaranteed to play, it was an easy choice for everyone else too. My agent, family, and some of my dad's friends started booking flights to be in Cincinnati in a few days.

My attitude and mental approach was so different this time around. I came to the realization that God had found a way to bless me five weeks ago without my even knowing it. I spent a lot of time thinking about my earlier promotion to the Cardinals, and the fact that I didn't play in that series against San Diego. I came to believe that: God had protected me from myself. I thought, "What if I had pitched well coming out of the bullpen in one or more of those games?" I might have branded myself a relief pitcher in the eyes of the Cardinals, and that would have forever altered the trajectory of my career. A more possible scenario prompted this question: "What if I had received an opportunity and pitched poorly?" Coming out of the bullpen was not a natural position for me. I may not have been as prepared as I normally would be. I could have easily been written off. Doubts could overcome encouragement, pessimism could replace optimism, and the narrative could have been, "He just couldn't overcome that injury." God didn't allow my story to be told in that way, and I was too wrapped up in prideful feelings of anger at the time to realize it.

Instead of a long drive north with Jenn, Casen, and Molly, the Cardinals flew my teammate and fellow pitcher Austin Gomber, who was also called up, and me to meet the team in Cincinnati. In first-class no less. Along with starting my first Major League Baseball game, that was another first for me that week. Gomber would start the game one night after me, but you wouldn't know a couple of Triple-A pitchers were heading to the big leagues judging by our demeanor on the plane. I was as loose as could be, not even thinking about what was coming up. Gomber and I played cards the entire flight, laughing and enjoying how far we had come from long bus rides throughout Texas, Oklahoma, Missouri, and Wisconsin. My life was a miracle. I was fourteen months removed from surviving a near-fatal injury. At that time, I had been broke, unmarried, living in sin, scared, and facing a completely unknown future. In just over a year, God had changed and improved nearly every aspect of my life.

As our plane landed at Cincinnati/Northern Kentucky International Airport, I didn't know that God wasn't close to being done with how far He planned on taking me.

CHAPTER 8

SPECIAL DAY;
SPECIAL PRAYER

The most important piece of equipment I travel with is lodged in my carry-on every single road trip. It's near me during homestands. I don't think I would have been drafted four times without it. I'm pretty certain I wouldn't be a player in Major League Baseball if I didn't use it. And I know for a fact that I wouldn't be alive if I didn't have it. It gives me the strength to be a professional athlete and the inspiration to be a good man. It's well-worn, marked up, and makes my eyes hurt sometimes. But now, particularly since my injury, I can't imagine going through a day without reading it. And July 23, 2018, was no different. I planned to read my Bible just like always on the day of my debut as a big league pitcher.

I had never been to Cincinnati, Ohio, prior to July 22, 2018, but it will always be a special place for me. I was drafted by the Reds in 2012, in the thirty-eighth round. Even though they must have believed that more than a thousand other players were better than me, it's flattering when a franchise shows its belief in you by calling your name in a draft. I didn't sign a professional contract with them; instead, I returned to college and transferred to the University of Houston. But the first morning I ever woke up in Cincinnati, the day just felt different. I was actually going to be starting a Major League Baseball game. It was my debut, and unlike the previous month, when the Cardinals called me up and kept me in the bullpen as insurance, I was going to be on the mound tonight for sure. That had already been decided. It was comforting to approach the day knowing I would finally have the chance to prove myself.

I had a little bit of jitteriness, not a terrible amount, but just enough to feel like you have an edge. As an athlete and competitor, you become used to that feeling, I think even more so if you are a pitcher and play only once every four or five days. I've heard that longtime veterans who have pitched in big games for years say they still experience it on days they pitch, and I welcomed it this morning. I didn't think about it at the time, but as I look back at this day, I feel now everything was determined by God. My slight case of nervous anticipation was probably a gift from Him as a way to keep focused on my job and not let my mind wander.

Superstitions are common in baseball, but I've never believed in them. I don't have any crazy quirks or special routines I follow on days I am going to pitch. There is no special meal I have to eat. No unusual or wacky way I put on my uniform. But, while I don't have superstitions, I do have a routine. It's an interesting life, playing a game every day for almost six months straight. I count on these routines to provide a sense of normalcy. Sometimes things become such a blur it's easy to forget what city you are in. That was not something I would have a problem with this day. The individual journey every player takes to eventually end up in the major leagues is challenging. That's what makes it so rewarding when you finally get there. My path took me through four colleges, five minor league towns, and the intensive care unit of a hospital. I planned to make this game day as ordinary as I could. At least that was my intent.

The problem was, nothing was routine on this surreal day. Starting with where I woke up. For the first time in my baseball career, I was in a luxury hotel with my teammates. Most visiting teams in Cincinnati stay at the Westin Hotel downtown, just blocks away from Great American Ball Park. That meant a number of perks I hadn't experienced in my five-plus seasons in the minor leagues. Dark, quiet rooms and comfortable beds. Numerous options for odd-hour meals. Creature comforts that allowed you to concentrate on your job.

Jenn and Casen drove with her dad from Memphis and met me at the hotel. Jenn and I both understood the importance of this day without needing to talk about it. Here we were, in a beautiful hotel room, about to experience a dream come true. We had both essentially dedicated our adult lives to this. Just fourteen months ago, as I lay in the ICU, we worried it would never happen. That reality was not lost on us. Back then, tying my own shoes felt like a miraculous gift. Now, here we were. Married, with Casen by our side and family and friends scattered around town, I was about to pitch in a game that night. This was a very big day. We both knew it, felt it, and tried our very best to ignore it.

Our families knew it too. They had mobilized quickly to make arrangements to get to Ohio to support me, and a group of at least ten of us gathered for breakfast. It would be the only time I could spend with them until after the game. I was grateful so many of them could make it. My sister, Bianca, and her husband drove all the way from Baltimore to be there. My dad flew in from California. A lot of Jenn's family and my agent came from Florida. This was a once-in-a-lifetime occasion for all of us, and since they had been right there with me for the hard times the year before, they wanted to be there for the first major-league game I was assured to play in. As our breakfast broke up and I attempted to pay for the meal, the waitress said, "Your bill has been taken care of." I took a look around the restaurant to see if I could recognize anyone and made eye contact with Matt Carpenter, one of the veterans and leaders on the team, and gave him a thankful wave. What an incredibly considerate thing to do. He didn't know me well, but he probably knew I hadn't thrown my first pitch as a major leaguer and wasn't consistently receiving a major league paycheck. A gesture like that from a class act like Matt was very much appreciated.

There is a lot of downtime in baseball, especially on the road, and I had a few hours to kill before heading to the stadium. It's funny, because people I talked to thought I would be obsessed with the magnitude of the game. What it signified. I understand why they thought that. I'm sure people were assuming I would be nervous, maybe overwhelmed by the moment. Fearful of something bad happening again. But I was really just locked in on the game and pitching well. Proving I belonged there. Winning.

Jenn was now accustomed to the drill of being a baseball wife, of having to be resourceful and finding things to do before going to the stadium. She had her own routine, and it usually included exploring a new city and walking around or doing a little shopping. The Cardinals, like most Major League Baseball teams, require players to be dressed respectably while traveling and when entering a stadium, as they represent the franchise. In the mad rush to get to Ohio, I had forgotten to bring a belt to wear to the game, so Jenn was going to see if she could find one. Who knew that would be so tough? There wasn't a single belt under $100 in any of the stores downtown. That kept her occupied, as did spending time with her family, but Jenn was still antsy. I could tell she was on edge by the mountain of clothes that had been thrown around the hotel room. It appeared she had sampled about a dozen outfit combinations before settling on the right thing to wear. Everyone copes with tension in his or her own way, and I'm just glad Jenn brought a big enough suitcase on this trip to deal with her tension.

With Jenn, Casen, and my family taken care of, I was able to have some time alone. The most important routine of my day is to find time to spend with God, and this was especially true on the day of my Major League Baseball debut. I like to read His Word, absorbing and really thinking about the Scriptures I am currently studying. On this morning, I couldn't have settled on a more perfect message. It was exactly what I needed at the moment. First Peter 5:6–7 says, "Humble yourselves, therefore, under God's mighty hand, that he may lift you up in due time. Cast all your anxiety on him because he cares for you." And as the day unfolded, I would need to call upon this exact message and words of encouragement on several occasions.

I let that short but powerful passage marinate as I reread it several times. Then I closed the book and continued that prayer with words of my own. I simply asked God for calmness and focus. Nothing more than that. I didn't ask to have a great game, or anything along those lines. I asked God for a way to allow me to glorify Him on this major league stage I was on. I knew a lot of attention would be given to me. The story of my injury was still so recent and fresh, even though in my mind, I had moved past it and was thinking about only my job that night. I wondered if people thought the Cardinals were giving me this chance because of it. And did the organization really believe I had the ability to stay at this level and contribute on a regular basis? I hoped so. No matter what I did in the game or how well it went, I was resigned to the fact that I would be interviewed.

My focus was on staying calm. Being focused and ready so I could give myself the best chance to showcase what I knew I was capable of doing. The better I pitched, the more attention I could bring to God. That was exactly what I prayed for, and that was precisely what God delivered to me.

Armed with the proper motivation, it was time to get ready to play the game I'd waited a lifetime to play. My mind and spirit were in the place they needed to be. Things had been happening at a whirlwind pace since the moment I was told I was being called up. I'd barely had enough time to pack and physically get to Cincinnati. (Without my belt.) Some pitchers are maniacal about their preparation, watching as much film as they can, consulting with advance scouts and the pitching coach, working out a meticulous strategy for each pitch in their mind. I've found the less I know about an opposing team the better, because that forces me to stick to my game plan and do what I do best. For the most part, I have only three pitches that I regularly use, and I know each day which one of them is working best. Location, changing speeds, and being consistent are the things I focus on in a game, and an overwhelming amount of data doesn't generally work to my advantage.

The only thing I really knew about this Reds team was that they had a pretty solid lineup from top to bottom. They were dangerous, with one great hitter, Joey Votto, in the middle of the order; and an old college teammate of mine at the University of Arizona, Brandon Dixon, batting second.

When it was time, I went downstairs, where there were two luxury coach buses at the front entrance of the hotel to take players, coaches, and support staff to the stadium. An unwritten baseball rule is that rookies take the first bus to the stadium, but on this day I violated it and boarded the second bus that left later. I wasn't trying to be defiant, I was simply hoping to stick with my typical game-day routine, and if I rode the bus departing first, I would have had a lot more downtime to kill. Nobody seemed to notice I wasn't wearing a belt.

Everything about this experience was new for me. It was the first time I had been on the road with the Cardinals, and the first time I would step foot inside this stadium. It took less than five minutes to arrive, and the first thing I wanted to do was get into the clubhouse, drop my bag off at my locker, and get the lay of the land. There was still a lot of time, four hours or so, before the start of the game, so there was no rush to learn the configurations of the tunnel and the route to the dugout and to the field. I like to walk on the field early in order to get a glimpse of what I'll be looking at from the mound. Every stadium has its own quirks and unique aspects. Up until this point in my career, I had played in only minor league ballparks that were a fraction of the size of this beautiful stadium.

One of the biggest perks of playing in the major leagues is that everything is prepared and taken care of. Players don't have to worry about anything except being ready to do their job. My uniform was perfectly pressed and hung in my locker. Music was playing in the background as my teammates were starting their various pregame rituals and routines. I checked out the weight room, which was much nicer and featured more machines than most of the health clubs I'd been to in the minor league cities where I lived.

Being hungry is something you don't ever have to worry about as a major leaguer. That's another thing that is taken care of, even for the visiting teams. I looked inside the kitchen to see what the cooks were preparing. There are always numerous options to choose from, many of them healthy and a far cry from what was served a generation ago as pregame meals. As the start of a game gets closer, I have a hard time eating. I just don't have an appetite, and I'd much rather pitch on an empty stomach as opposed to the alternative. I took a few bites of lunch to get some fuel in me and continued to check out my surroundings.

I had not been around my Cardinals teammates a lot since I

was just joining the team, but we had all been together in Florida back in spring training. I had discovered that there were other believers on the team. Great Christian guys like Mike Mayers and Adam Wainwright. And of course Matt Carpenter, who had paid for our breakfast. I thanked him again when I saw him. "Good luck tonight," he told me. Mayers gave me a hug and wished me well.

As a rookie pitcher trying to figure things out in his first game, I was fortunate to have a built-in advantage that automatically came with playing for the St. Louis Cardinals. Yadier Molina had been the Cardinals catcher since I was in the seventh grade. The most respected and knowledgeable catcher in baseball, he had won two World Series, a World Baseball Classic with Puerto Rico, and appeared in more MLB All-Star Games (9) than days I had even been on an MLB roster (4). And that was counting this day. He was a star, a walking baseball historian and tactical strategist, and probably the best catcher any rookie making his debut could ask to have behind the plate. What makes him even more unique and special to me is that he didn't take offense when I presented my thoughts for a strategy against the Reds hitters that night. I walked up to one of the best catchers of our generation as he watched film of the Reds pitcher we would be facing that night, said "Hello," and then got right down to business.

"How do you want to throw today?" he asked me.

"I'd like to stick with three pitches," I replied. "Primarily fastballs." I even told him how I wanted him to position himself behind the plate. I knew he didn't know much, if anything, about me, but being the consummate professional that he is, he was open to my input. So I let him know what had worked best for me in the minor leagues. He listened to my suggestions and we bantered a little more about the game plan. He was a crafty veteran who had literally seen nearly every possible situation in baseball. I was a raw, inexperienced rookie, navigating a clubhouse for the first time as a starting pitcher. He most likely wanted to make sure I was as comfortable as I could be. It's one of the qualities that makes him such a great catcher. When it comes to pitching strategy, it's all about making sure the pitcher is in a comfort zone. There was no reason for him to bombard me with information that would either confuse me or be forgotten by the time I got to the mound that night.

That calm, cool, and collected approach of Yadi suited me perfectly. Elaborate game plans aren't typically my thing, and I want information about opposing hitters only if it is ultra-important, something I don't know, or something I can really use to my advantage in the game. For the most part, I like to pitch to my strength and go from there. As the clock inched closer to the local start time of 7:10 eastern, I was feeling good both physically and mentally. I wasn't overwhelmed. My mind wasn't filled with any sort of fear or apprehension; in fact, it was just the opposite.

I put on my uniform. I sometimes get comments about the height of my pants. Simply put, I jack my pants up pretty high, and I realize I look at times like I have stepped out of another era, with high funky pants and my glasses. The glasses are gone now, thanks to the Lasik surgery I had in 2019. But there's no surgery that can get me to wear my pants down by my ankles. They are going to stay up high.

To almost everyone else in the clubhouse, this game was nothing more than another matchup in the hot and monotonous dog days of summer. It was just one of the nineteen times these two teams would face off during the season. Game number 100 of 162 for both clubs. Clearly, the game was much more important for me, but I could not allow that fact to affect my thoughts or actions. I needed to show my teammates that I could handle the moment. Luckily, it wasn't an act. I was still feeling calm, armed with the words of the prayer in the morning and the message of the Bible passage I'd read still with me. God granted me the peace and calmness I needed. There's no way I could have pitched to my potential that night if I had allowed the moment to be bigger than it was. God kept me from acting as if this were anything out of the ordinary. I'm grateful for that, because if I'd let my mind wander and started buying into some dramatic narrative, I would have been in trouble. Big trouble. In baseball we have a crude but accurate phrase for that: tight butthole. No need for further explanation. We keep things simple, to the point, and sometimes, unfortunately, colorful in clubhouse terminology.

I checked the clock on the wall. It was time to warm up. I went to the field with a handful of my teammates. I started stretching and doing my dynamic warm-up that included short running bursts, some jumping, and a couple of other exercises designed to get my heart rate up and loosen my joints and muscles.

As I started my routine that night, my head was filled with songs from my playlist of worship music. I headed to the field with my earphones on, continuing my mental preparation by listening to music from Hillsong UNITED and a few other groups. My go-to songs before every game include Hillsong's "When I Lost My Heart to You," "Hallelujah," and "Prince of

Peace." They are the backdrop to my normal warm-up routine and preparation, and they sounded even more inspiring and uplifting than usual to me on this day.

I like to absorb powerful messages before a game. "Jesus, You make the darkness tremble" is from the song "Tremble" by Mosaic MSC. That's the kind of music I want to listen to and have in my ear. At the end of my playlist, there's a song by a group named Shane & Shane called "Psalm 34." I love the words, the message, and the melody of that song. It was everything I needed in a moment like this, and the perfect complement to my special morning prayer.

> *I sought the Lord*
> *and He answered me*
> *and delivered me*
> *from every fear...*

As the next several hours played out, the words of that song turned out to be incredibly prophetic. I ended the warm-up drill jogging by myself to an area in center field where I could be alone for a minute. I needed to compose and collect myself one final time. I knelt down, closed my eyes, and said one last prayer. I could feel the warm sun on me, and the smell of the outfield grass had the unmistakable aroma of summer, of base-ball. The cavernous stadium was still essentially empty, but there was a palpable buzz beginning to register in the air. I felt so incredibly blessed at that moment. So grateful for the oppor-tunity God had given me. I was determined to do anything I possibly could to pay Him back, and I repeated the same mes-sage I had prayed in the morning. I asked God one more time to provide me a sense of calm and allow me to use my talents to bring Him glory.

I jumped to my feet and headed to play catch with bullpen catcher Jamie Pogue. We started with warm-up tosses, then increased the distance between us, then brought it back to ninety feet. I began throwing some of the pitches I would be using in the game. I started with some off-speed stuff, then a cutter, fol-lowed by a changeup. I tried a curveball to see if I had it for the night and if it might be a pitch I would feel comfortable using. I didn't. The four-seam fastball would be my primary pitch, and Yadi and I would weave in the others to hopefully keep the Cin-cinnati batters guessing.

Things had progressed normally, and I was almost com-pletely done with my warm-up in the outfield. The next thing would be some real pitches in the bullpen, and then it was showtime. My arm felt great. Mentally, I was focused and excited. The sound of my fastball popping into Pogue's leather catcher's mitt cut through the air. My ball was alive. Physically, I was ready. The adrenaline of being in this big-time environment seemed to add a mile or two per hour to the velocity of my pitches. The only thing left to do was to throw one more warm-up pitch in the outfield. The most routine, insignificant part of pregame activity. It's called a "long toss," meaning I'm not quite simulating an actual pitch in a game condition. On my final throw, I would always dig deep and find a little extra on this last fastball. I equate this to cracking a whip. I wanted to uncork one final heater; then, I would be done warming up. Just one last pitch.

I threw the ball, and I instantaneously knew something was wrong. The ball sank into Pogue's glove at the same moment I reached up to grab the side of my neck. A piercing pain and burning sensation moved from the top of my shoulder into the side of my neck. I rotated my neck from side to side. At least I tried to do that. I could not move my neck laterally at all. Less than an hour before the most important game of my professional career, I couldn't turn my head to face home plate.

This wasn't the first time I had tweaked my neck during or prior to a game, but it had never been this bad, and it had never been this close to the start of the first inning. I tried to play it cool and walked to the bullpen. I was hoping I could work it out by continuing to throw in my bullpen session, but no such luck. I started spiking pitches left and right. I was so far off the plate it was ridiculous. The Cardinals pitching coach Mike Maddux was watching me warm up, and he must have thought I was having a nervous breakdown. He and our bullpen coach were standing to the side, no doubt wondering what the heck was wrong with me. Yadi Molina was there too. There wasn't much he hadn't seen in his seventeen-year career in baseball, but this might have fallen into that rare category.

At that point, nobody had said a word. But if I hadn't given them enough proof that something weird was going on, I solid-ified the message on the next pitch I threw. The curveball I tried to get *across* the plate instead bounced five feet in *front* of the plate. It hit the bullpen catcher in the mask, shot straight up in the air, and clanked off an overhang directly above us in the visitors' bullpen. Now my goal was simply not to hurt anybody else. Maddux said, "Hey, is everything okay?"

"I think I tweaked my neck," I replied. I wouldn't have blamed Yadi, Maddux, and Pogue if they'd thought I was freak-ing out or letting my nerves get the best of me. But it was just that I was in pain, and I had no mobility in my neck whatsoever.

The singer of the national anthem had taken the field and

was holding the microphone. This game was minutes from starting. If I couldn't find a way to work this kink out of my neck very soon, I was not going to be able to pitch.

But the power of prayer and my faith in God's healing grace had allowed me to survive something much more serious than this just over a year ago. I had asked God to allow me to stay calm on this day, and I repeated those words to Him in a silent prayer as I turned to our pitching coach and said, "Mike, can you come here for a second?"

CHAPTER 9

A MAGICAL NIGHT IN CINCINNATI

I didn't stand for the national anthem prior to my Major League Baseball debut. I sure wish I had been able to, but the massive kink in my neck prevented it. This was the eightieth start of my professional career, and I was more physically limited than I had ever been prior to throwing my first pitch. I've had sore shoulders and normal wear-and-tear aggravations, but what I was feeling was different. Mike Maddux joined me in a side room just outside the bullpen as the anthem was playing, and I had him drive his elbow into my neck as hard as he could, hoping it would loosen me up. I laid down on a baseball and tried to roll the ball through the kink. The anthem ended and the crowd cheered just as I walked out of the side room and back to the bullpen mound. I took a deep breath, rotated my neck to see if the pain had subsided, and fired a few more pitches. None of them were disasters, and a couple of them were strikes, so I declared myself ready to go. It was my only choice.

The game started and I headed back into the clubhouse to have my trainer, Chris Conroy, do some last-second work on me that gave me just enough neck rotation to see home plate. I maximized every second I had. I took some ibuprofen and rubbed Icy Hot into my skin, which ultimately made things worse, because when you sweat it magnifies the intensity of the heat. So now, I had burning skin covering my locked-up neck. There was nothing left to do at this point. I had to take the mound and just deal with it. The more relaxed I could force myself to be, the better.

Thankfully, the prayer I had said worked, because I was extremely calm considering the circumstances. I was so calm, in fact, that I didn't even take a moment to soak in the scenery, partly because I couldn't get my neck to move enough to scan the surroundings.

Jenn later told me that she had looked around and taken it all in. After watching countless games as my girlfriend, Jenn was enjoying her first season as my wife. The peace, comfort, and confidence that come with being married made such a difference for her, and unlike me, she *was* able to appreciate the surroundings. For her, it put into perspective how far I and everyone around me had come since I was in that hospital room in Des Moines. She describes watching me on the mound, under those lights, with all eyes focused on me, as being *surreal*. It was humbling to later learn how emotional my family and friends became as they watched me that night. Both Jenn and my agent, Brian Grieper, told me there wasn't a dry eye among them as they each reflected on how much I had gone through to get to this point. It wasn't just the near-death experience the previous season, but all the challenges I faced in the minor leagues and colleges along the way. I had an incredible group of supporters, and I was grateful they would actually be watching me pitch, unlike those three games in St. Louis a month ago when I never left the bullpen. They were in their seats, and it was time for me to take the ball and go to work.

On this night, none of the backstory mattered. I would be judged solely on how I performed against big league competition, and it was finally my time to seize the moment and prove what I'd never doubted—I belonged there. My neck was still very tight, but having to zero in on my catcher Yadi's sign and focus on the batter provided the distraction I desperately needed.

José Peraza led off for the Reds in the bottom of the first. My strategy for the game was simple: I would throw fastballs, cutters, and changeups. Exclusively. I had no intent of trying to get fancy or try to outthink Yadi, who had the equivalent of a Harvard PhD when it came to handling pitchers. Whatever sign he put down, I was going with it. A fastball. I took one final breath, gripped the ball inside my glove, and set out to officially change my story. I launched the four-seam fastball and it broke all the way across the plate. Yadi caught the ball as the leather of his mitt snapped in the silence of this Cincinnati evening. He framed the ball on the edge of the strike zone.

"Ball," the home plate umpire barked out as he leaned slightly to get a better view.

I was hoping he had seen it as a strike, but regardless, I was off and running, and the pregame butterflies that I'd had most of the day were gone. They literally disappeared, just like that. I calmed down even further and locked in on Peraza, and he lined out to right on a routine play. One down.

Next up for the Reds was Brandon Dixon, my freshman roommate at the University of Arizona. I got him to line out to left, which then brought Joey Votto to the plate. He was a star for the Reds and one of their biggest offensive threats. I knew he would punish me for any mistake I made, so I was careful not to groove Votto anything he could mash, and he grounded out to second base. It was a clean first inning. I retired the side 1-2-3, an ideal way to start. I left the mound feeling confident and relaxed.

I could tell early that the pace of the game was going to be brisk. We had gone down in order in the first inning, and as I was getting worked on in the clubhouse in the top of the second, José Martinez singled for our first hit of the game. But we didn't score. And just like that I was walking back to the mound. I recorded my very first strikeout to start the bottom of the second. After the third strike was called, Yadier Molina rolled the ball into the dugout for our clubhouse attendant to grab and present to me at the end of the game. He had done the same thing with my first pitch of the game, and I gave one of those balls to my dad and the other to my wife.

The next batter for the Reds flew out to center, and I followed that with a two-out walk to Tucker Barnhart. The walk didn't faze me. I walk a lot of batters. Always have. I had to make sure I didn't open the floodgates with another walk, so I reared back and put a little extra gas on my fastball and got Adam Duvall to strike out, swinging on a pitch that was up and away, ending the inning. I walked to the dugout feeling good because I could tell my fastball was working. I knew it by the amount of swings and misses I was getting. If I pitch well, then it's because my fastball is really effective. I remember thinking as I made my way to the dugout that it was especially crisp on this night.

I was due to come to the plate and hit in the top of the third. I had a simple game plan for what I would do when I was at the plate: not swing the bat. Seriously, my intent was to not take the bat off my shoulder for two reasons. One, I wasn't what you would call an offensive threat. I had almost no chance of getting a hit that night. Two, swinging the bat could actually amplify the kink in my neck, so I was a casual observer as Reds pitcher Luis Castillo painted three fastballs down and away. I walked back to the dugout after looking at a called third strike.

Because the game was moving along quickly, I had little time to think about what was transpiring. As soon as I removed my helmet and took a seat on the bench, it was time to go back out for the bottom of the third. At this point my neck was mostly a nonfactor. Maybe there was some residual by-product of that kink that actually forced me to focus even more than usual. The only thing that mattered was that I have another smooth inning and retire the side in order. I had made it through three innings without giving up a hit or a run. It was a decent start, but I still had a long way to go. The pregame adrenaline had worn off by this point, and I could have used a cup of coffee. I turned to my buddy Jack Flaherty on the bench and asked him for a favor. "Could you run into the clubhouse and grab me a coffee, Jack? Maybe put some ice in it?" I requested.

"No problem," he replied. "I got you." It was as simple as ordering a drink at Starbucks, and a nice perk you won't find in lower-level minor league ball. Shortly after that, I was treated to another big league perk that changed the narrative of the game. My old college roommate Brandon Dixon led off the fourth by smoking a 95 mph fastball that I grooved right over the heart of the plate. It was a rocket, on its way to the wall, and by the time I was able to turn my head and see where it landed, our right fielder Dexter Fowler had also turned and started to monitor the flight of the ball. He pivoted, took five measured steps to prepare for a leaping catch if necessary, and at the last moment, reached his left glove as high as he could to snare the ball in midair. It was a fantastic defensive play by one of the best right fielders in baseball. Without question it would have been a double for Brandon if Dex had not made that incredible play, and the story of the night would have been written much differently. I offered a small thanks to God, walked the next batter, then recorded two outs to end the inning. The first thing I did when the inning was over was to find Fowler in the dugout and thank him for making such a fantastic play.

I knew that I was under a pitch count of roughly one hundred that night, but because I didn't get into any serious jams, I was cruising along. My arm felt strong, and the kink in my neck was officially a moot point. Fans of baseball know that it is an incredibly superstitious sport. There are phrases that are taboo to verbalize, or even bring up during a game. Let's just say I was in the middle of one of those unmentionable situations. Specifically, I had not allowed a hit in four innings of play. It was still early, but I did have a no-hitter in progress. My teammates were well aware of it, which meant, for the most part, they weren't talking to me between innings. I'm not a very talkative person myself in a game anyway, so that was actually okay. Fans who were watching the game on TV back in St. Louis who didn't know much about me may have been surprised at how relaxed I appeared. When I saw the replay of the game, I had this look of peace and a complete lack of visible stress that may have seemed abnormal for someone making his Major League Baseball debut. I had specifically prayed for peace and calmness before the game, and it was visually clear to anyone watching that God was providing both for me.

In the stands where my family was sitting, things were festive and electric as the magnitude of what was occurring became more widely known and appreciated. It was hard for them not to be excited at how the game was progressing, yet they knew the importance of it for me and felt some of the same intensity I felt.

My dad's demeanor is the complete opposite of mine. He's the life of the party. He's animated, and even more so when things are going well for me. He very much made his presence felt on this night, wearing a red Cardinals polo shirt and black Cardinals hat. Jenn has the perfect way to describe my dad's antics during a game: "appropriately loud." He'll whistle and scream and make a scene one moment, but he knows when to tone it down too. Jim Hayes, one of the announcers for the Fox Sports Midwest broadcast team that carries the Cardinals games in St. Louis, knew exactly where my dad was seated, and he was determined to interview him during the game.

"Can we talk to you, Mr. Poncedeleon?" Hayes asked.

"Look, I'm just a dad. You have to interview Daniel," my dad told him.

"No, we want to interview you because of his injury, Mr. Poncedeleon. Fans would love to hear from you," Hayes followed up.

"But I don't want to be interviewed. I'm not ready," Dad said. The combination of my agent, Brian, encouraging my dad to do the interview, and the fact that Jim Hayes was persistent and did not leave the area for an inning and a half, convinced my dad to do the interview. He performed great on-camera. He wanted to convey his gratitude to God for bringing me back and providing this magical moment. He was so thankful to the Cardinals for all they had done, and he wanted to thank all the fans who had prayed for me, he said, because those prayers were real and they had been answered. I don't think my dad actually said all of that, although he wanted to, and he has mentioned a variation of it in almost every interview he's done since.

There was another moment that night that led my family to believe something special might be happening. A foul ball came incredibly close to where they were sitting, landing just two rows away from them in the exact same section. The fan who caught the foul ball knew it was my family sitting together watching my debut, so he gave the foul ball to my dad.

It had the makings of a magical night, but in reality, there still was plenty of work to do. One mistake could turn things south, so I stayed with the philosophy of focusing on one pitch at a time. The Reds hitters were beginning to face me for the second and third time. I would have to be exceptionally crafty since they had seen my stuff for the past ninety minutes of play. Big league hitters are experts at making in-game adjustments at the plate, and I had to counter that with even more effective pitches to try to keep them off-balance. I needed the velocity of my fastball to stay in the mid-90s. If it dipped, I was in trouble. One thing that guarantees a pitcher staying locked in is a pitching duel, and I was in the midst of one. Luis Castillo was tossing a great game for the Reds, and neither team had yet to score a run. We went up and down with three quick outs in the top of the fifth inning without scoring. I arrived on the mound in the bottom of the fifth looking to show Mike Shildt, who'd become the new Cardinals manager earlier in the month, that I was not losing steam. My fastball was still around 96 mph on the radar gun, and I retired the Reds 1-2-3 with a fly ball to the outfield, a pop fly to the infield, and a ground ball right back to me that I easily threw to first for the out. The Reds had yet to record a base hit. We had just two hits in this scoreless game, and I felt that if our offense could get me one or two runs, I would hold the lead.

Our offense delivered in the sixth. Matt Carpenter led off the inning with a double, and Yadier Molina drove him home with a single. We struck quickly, and it was 1–0. My dad and our rooting section were whooping it up, and I shot to my feet to congratulate Carpenter as he came back into the dugout after scoring the first run. I now had the chance to be the winning pitcher. If I could do my job for a few more innings and hold this lead, I would record my very first "W" (win) in my very first start.

The one-run lead had given me a burst, and I pulled the string on Billy Hamilton to lead off the bottom of the sixth with a strikeout. The Reds were at the top of their lineup now, and I continued to keep them off balance. José Peraza flew out to left, and Brandon Dixon grounded out to short. I had now pitched six full innings and had yet to give up a hit or a run. The stonewalling in the dugout was in full force as we batted in the seventh. Nobody wanted to talk to me, sit by me, or do anything that could be deemed responsible for jinxing what I was in the process of doing.

My mom does not fly, so she was not at this game in person. My dad has a travel buddy from work named George Salas whom he calls his "road dog." About this time in the game, George committed the cardinal sin of saying out loud what was obvious to everybody, the fact that I had not given up a hit yet. I had three innings to go, but I was throwing a no-hitter.

"Hey!" he announced to those around him as I was walking to the dugout. "Daniel has a no-hitter going!" My dad, along with his friend Freddie Luevanos, elbowed George in the ribs and pounced on his violation of the unwritten rule. "You don't say that until after the game!" my dad yelled at him.

I'm the type of pitcher who can go deep into counts and I have a tendency to walk batters, which means my pitch count is generally on the high side. In games like these, managers are forced to make very tough decisions. They must decide to either remove pitchers in the midst of no-hitters to protect their arm for the rest of the season, or let it ride and see if the pitcher can make history. I didn't give it any thought, and, realistically, I felt I had two or three more innings left where I could continue to pitch this effectively. If I got wild and started walking batters or my fastball velocity went down and the Reds started pounding me, then it would be an easy decision for my manager to make.

I asked God to be with me as I grabbed my glove and walked to the mound with a 1–0 lead and a pitch count creeping toward triple digits. My body was telling me I was nearing the end, but I remember thinking I had at least one more good inning left in the tank. I started the seventh inning facing Joey Votto for the third time. I walked him, putting myself in an immediate jam. I knew if I walked or gave up a hit to the batter coming up, I would probably get a visit to the mound from my pitching coach, and my manager would be placing a call to the bullpen for a reliever to get loose. This was an extremely critical moment in the game, and while Eugenio Suárez drove a pitch fairly deep to left, it was easily caught for an out. That changed everything, because now a ground ball could get me out of the inning if we turned a double play.

Jesse Winker came up next and sent a short fly ball to left that Marcell Ozuna hauled in effortlessly again. Now there were two outs. Tucker Barnhart was up next. I took a peek at Votto, making sure he wasn't getting too big of a lead at first, and fired a changeup that Barnhart got underneath, sending another harmless fly ball to shallow left that Ozuna corralled for the third out. The Reds had fouled off a lot of my pitches in that inning. My fastball was still hitting at 96 mph on the gun, but my off-speed pitches weren't as sharp as they had been earlier. I got myself out of the seventh inning, but as I walked off the mound, I was upset with myself. I knew I got away with one against Barnhardt in that last at bat. At that moment, Yadier Molina started walking toward me instead of going straight to the dugout.

"Man, that last pitch sucked," I remember telling my catcher. I shook my head in frustration while he shook my hand in congratulations. I was mad at myself for making a bad pitch, even though it didn't lead to any damage. I remember letting out a deep breath. Almost like I was exhaling after holding air in my lungs for the past fourteen months. A rush of thoughts bombarded my mind, and one of them was to look up for the first time the entire game and glance at the stands. I wanted to see if I could find my family. In doing that, I realized in my mind the night was over and I would not return to the game. My manager confirmed that when I reached the dugout steps. Mike Shildt met me with his hand outstretched.

"Great job," he told me. "That's it."

I have to admit I wondered whether I should lobby to stay in the game. I smartly decided that was not a good idea for someone making his first start in the big leagues and who had just thrown 116 pitches. My spot in the lineup was coming up, and with me being an offensive liability in a tight game, I had no problem accepting my manager's decision. I paused for a second, then simply said, "All right."

After that, my Cardinals teammates hustled over to congratulate me, shaking my hand and giving me hugs. All of them said, "Great job." It was such a gratifying feeling to pitch well for these guys and have them appreciate it. I found a place on the dugout bench where I could be alone. I was so grateful. Not for what I had done, but for what God had just *allowed* me to do. I covered my face, and for the first time all day, I allowed myself to show a little emotion as a couple of tears trickled down my cheek.

My feelings at that moment were a combination of joy, gratefulness, and relief. I knew in my heart I was ready for my moment, and I had seen time and again how God could work miracles in my life. But I still had not been expecting this. I threw seven innings of no-hit, shutout ball. MLB.com later referred to it as the third-greatest debut for a pitcher in Major League Baseball history. It's hard for me to comprehend that even now as I think about those words. The Elias Sports Bureau said it was only the fifth time a pitcher took a no-hitter this deep into a game in his debut since the expansion era began in 1961. For me, the game felt like it was the World Series. The reason I play so hard is because I just want to win, so even though my job was done and we led 1–0, we needed to hold the lead against a good team. We still had to win the game. Winning really meant that much to me, and I desperately wanted my performance to have contributed to a victory.

The combined no-hitter for our pitching staff was no longer a possibility when the Reds got their first hit in the eighth inning. In the ninth inning, our closer, Bud Norris, came in to hopefully slam the door. We were up 1–0, and Bud actually got the first two batters out in the ninth. We were one out away from winning the game, Bud was pitching well, but the Reds simply got to him on this night. They finished with a flurry, registering a home run, two singles, a walk and then a walk-off single to end the game. We lost 2–1. The game ended so abruptly I was kind of in shock, but I made sure I didn't display any disappointment on my face. I was as stoic as I could possibly be. As the Reds started jumping around and celebrating at home plate, I walked into the clubhouse as casually as I could. I received more congratulations in the clubhouse, which felt a little odd because we didn't *win* the game, but something very special happened after we had all showered and changed clothes. I was walking out to do an interview when Bud Norris came up to me, still sweating, and still dressed in most of his uniform.

"I'm sorry, man," he told me, looking sincerely bummed. "I didn't know what had happened to you last year."

"Thank you, Bud," I said, and told him to not worry about it. "I'll have a lot more opportunities."

I felt as bad for Bud because of how hard he was taking it as he felt for me. He even went so far as to speak very encouraging words about me to the media. "It was incredible," he told Fox Sports Midwest, describing my performance. "He was in control the whole way. This is a tough ballpark to pitch in, and it was an incredible debut. Obviously, I'm pretty bummed that I didn't get it done for him, but it's a big statement for him, one that he can build on from here and something he will never forget."

Being sought out by the national media after a game had not been part of my postgame minor league routine in State College, Springfield, Palm Beach, or Memphis. But a lot of people wanted to talk to me after this game, and the Cardinals PR director approached me in the clubhouse to tell me I was wanted on the field.

"Could you hold on for just a second?" I asked him. "I want to say hi to my family first if I can."

I walked outside the clubhouse to the tunnel in the bowels of Great American Ball Park to say hi to everybody who had come to watch me. There's no way to put into words how special that moment was, seeing the pride and joy on the faces of my family and Jenn's family, as well as my dad's friends and my agent, Brian. It was an incredible moment, so warm and loving. Everyone hugged and kissed me. We made plans to meet up after I had completed the interviews, and I went back into the clubhouse and then onto the field to do the first one. The MLB Network connected me remotely with their studio hosts in Seacaucus, New Jersey, and I was stunned and thrilled when

I heard in my ear the voice of a pitcher I consider to be one of the greatest of all time. He told me he was impressed with the poise I showed in the game, and he asked me how I was able to appear so calm. It was Hall of Fame legend Pedro Martinez, and I shared my secret weapon with him. "Before the game I just prayed for some calm and focus," I told Pedro, wearing a headset and dress shirt while standing in a darkened stadium outside the visitors' dugout.

Following my injury the previous May, my story had received a great deal of media coverage, mostly because of the dramatic nature of the video. It aired for days, or so I was told. This was the first time I would be seen by a large national audience in a positive light for what I had accomplished, and I wanted to use this forum to make sure I was praising God and putting my Christian faith on display so people knew where my strength came from. Dan Plesac of the MLB Network was in the studio that evening with Pedro. He asked me if I thought my career might have been over after I was hit in the head.

"No," I told him. "Getting hit by that line drive changed my life. It allowed me to get closer to God and more involved in His Word." I made a point to answer the questions in that way because that's certainly how I felt, and I believed it was my responsibility to share this in the highest-profile way I could. God used me in that game to share the message I delivered. I wanted people to hear about the source of my strength.

There would be more interviews to do after the game, including one the following morning for CNN. I traveled to a downtown Cincinnati studio, sat in front of a green screen, and talked to the hosts of its morning program about the game and the details of returning from my injury.

I received so many texts and well-wishes after the game— literally hundreds. It took days for me to respond to all of them, and I tried to thank everybody who reached out. One of the most special messages came from the Cardinals scout who drafted me, Charlie Gonzalez. He called me after the game to tell me how proud he was of me, and then, just like he always had, he hung up before I could say good-bye. It had been a little over four years since I played my final year of college baseball in Florida, back when Charlie would be in touch with me multiple times a week. He believed I had Major League Baseball ability all along, but I'm not sure if he could have imagined my first game would go like this.

After the interviews ended, I met up with Jenn, along with her dad, my dad, my dad's friends, and my agent, Brian, for dinner at a little spot near the stadium called Condado Tacos. The big-screen television inside the restaurant was showing a replay of the game. Adding to the surreal aspect of the entire evening, I watched myself pitch while celebrating with my family. It was now getting late, but it felt like we needed to cap off the evening in a special way. So I invited everyone to my hotel room so I could show them what the accommodations were like now that I had made it to the big leagues for at least a couple of days. I had packed something special with me on this trip I wanted to share, and this was the perfect time to do it. When I was called up to the Cardinals a few weeks earlier, Brian had sent me a bottle of Dom Perignon champagne to celebrate the occasion. Since I didn't pitch in that series, the bottle had never been opened. I brought it with me to Ohio and had it tucked away in the room, and we decided to celebrate with a toast right there in the hotel. This was also my debut of opening a champagne bottle, and to be honest, it didn't go as well as my other debut that night. I had no clue how to pop it, and the cork rocketed to the ceiling. Thankfully, this *was* a no-hitter; no one was hit or injured.

I've been asked many times if I was surprised that I pitched so well in my debut. The answer I always give is that I knew I belonged in the big leagues. I knew my stuff would be effective, and I knew I had the ability to be a good Major League Baseball pitcher. Could I fathom I would throw seven no-hit innings this soon? In some ways, humbly, yes. I expected to go out and perform exceptionally well—I hold myself to that type of standard. The moment wasn't too big for me, and I wasn't scared. In the end, what I was truly hoping for was that the Cardinals would feel as an organization that I belonged with them. That I had erased any doubts that I belonged at the highest level of baseball.

Even though I received a lot of attention after the game and had pitched as best I could, realistically, there wasn't a short- or long-term spot on the roster for me at that time. I would have to be that guy sent back to Triple-A. And it happened soon. Real soon. After breakfast the following morning, my cell phone rang. I looked down, and on the screen was the name that made my stomach drop a little. Mike Shildt. He told me in a very nice and professional way that I was going back to Memphis, but he was looking forward to seeing me again soon. I was looking forward to that, too, and maybe even staying awhile next time.

CHAPTER 10

BACK TO REALITY

Ups and downs. Peaks and valleys. Bumps in the road. Elation, frustration, rejection, dejection. Any and all of those words describe my college and professional careers. The situation I was in now was no different. Major success one night, back to the minors the next morning. I had accepted that this was my narrative. A part of who I was. God chose this path for me, just like He chose every step beforehand. After receiving the news that I was going back to Memphis, I had an underlying feeling of anger that lingered with me for the next day. It wasn't a surprise I was going down, and I knew there was a lot involved in making these decisions. It was out of my control, but I was still angry about it. Not at any person, just the situation. But when I returned to Tennessee, I eventually replaced the anger with gratitude. I had just proven I had the talent to be a full-time Major League Baseball player. I had survived a near-death experience to come back against all odds and not only play baseball again, but also to have a special major league debut. Jenn and I were happily married with a healthy son and a daughter on the way. Just as importantly, I had a new platform to touch people and hopefully to help and inspire others. I told everyone I talked to and who would listen that nothing I'd accomplished would have been possible without God. I was grateful, and I was determined to show that what had just happened in Cincinnati wasn't a fluke.

My teammates in Memphis were awesome. As a minor leaguer, it's natural to get a little jealous when someone else is promoted, because you wish it had been you. At the same time, you're rooting for that player to crush it when they go up, because you've seen what your teammates have gone through and worked for to get to that point. I received nothing but heartfelt excitement and congratulations from the guys when they greeted me. My stay in Memphis would be short, because less than a week later, I was called up to St. Louis again. The team needed depth in the bullpen for a series versus the Colorado Rockies. We hosted the Rockies on Monday, July 30. It was a cool night by St. Louis standards, with a game-time tempera-ture of just 77 degrees. I loosened up a little before the game, then settled into the bullpen to watch. Carlos Martinez was our starting pitcher, but in the fourth inning, he suffered an injury and had to leave the game immediately. There were two Rock-ies on the bases when the bullpen phone rang. "Tell Ponce he's going in the game," was the message.

"What?" I replied when I was told that. "Me?" I was sur-prised and a little panicked by the call. When a pitcher is hurt, a reliever immediately comes in from the bullpen, so he has to warm up quickly. I jogged to the mound, as nervous as I have ever been in a baseball game, my heart beating through my chest. The unfamiliarity alone was intense. I had never come into a game as a reliever before, let alone where I had to warm up on the game mound in front of the entire stadium instead of in the bullpen as usual. I'm sure the Cardinals were hoping I would eat some innings because of the unplanned injury, so I tried to get as loose as I could, but all eyes from the crowd watching me warm up while the game was on pause was a whole other level of tension. I then turned around and analyzed what I faced: runners at second and third. I had inherited a bona fide jam. I walked the first batter, which loaded the bases and put me in a deeper hole. Waiting in the on-deck circle was one of five people on the entire planet a pitcher would least like to see in this situation: Nolan Arenado. The Rockies third baseman was one of the most feared hitters in baseball, a perennial all-star and legitimate superstar. At this point in my major league career, I had still not given up a hit, let alone a run, home run, or anything worse. I got ahead in the count with strike one against Arenado and started to feel confident. So far, so good. The next pitch I threw was also a strike. The difference this time, however, was that he took a swing and blasted it over the center-field wall for a grand slam. I had just given up my first hit, first run, first home run, and first grand slam. All in one swing. Less than a week before, I had been riding an ultimate high, but now I was standing all alone on the mound as four Rockies paraded around the bases and met at home plate to celebrate. As dramatic as it was, I didn't lose any confidence. I wasn't shaken. Arenado is a great hitter, and he beat me that time. I pitched a couple more innings, didn't give up another run, struck out two, and we came back to win the game 5–4.

The summer of 2018 included numerous trips to and from St. Louis. In August, I appeared in five games for the Cardinals, and four more in the month of September when the rosters were expanded to forty players. The back-and-forth trips were challenging professionally, but the upside was that at least I was earning enough money to survive and support my family.

Besides a positive balance in my bank account, I noticed something else while I was with the Cardinals. My profile had risen in St. Louis. There were now people interested in my autograph, and I was recognized in the city when I was at a restaurant. I would also hear a lot of references to the "Fountain of Youth," as fans drew the correlation between my name and the famous Spanish conquistador Juan Ponce de León. No relation, at least that I'm aware of.

With a more stable foundation in my personal and professional life, my spiritual life also improved. I developed a schedule of Bible study and prayer that I still follow in my daily routine today. I met a man by the name of Don Christensen at what's called PAO, Pro Athletes Outreach, a Christian retreat. Jenn and I attend annually in the off-season. Don developed a daily reading plan for the entire year, which included one reading each from the Old Testament, the New Testament, and a psalm or proverb. In the off-season of 2017, I started to receive invitations to speak to church groups throughout Florida about my life and faith, and I was asked to appear on Christian podcasts around the country. On social media, I kept my "direct message" option open on Twitter and allowed fans to directly communicate with me, and many of them posed questions about my faith. People all over the country and the world had seen and heard about my story and began reaching out. I was determined to respond to every message, knowing that just replying was sometimes enough to boost the spirits of people who were hurting or looking for encouragement. The media were more interested in what I had to say too. My opportunity to try to make a difference in the world presented itself, and I felt a calling to do what I could. I didn't look at it as my responsibility, but something that organically developed. I almost always mentioned the Lord in some way, shape, or form when I was interviewed. My daily readings provided a strong faith-based routine for my day and were responsible for the daily blessings I was receiving in my life.

A highlight of the 2018 season occurred on August 21. I was with the Cardinals on a road trip to the West Coast, and I made a start in Los Angeles against the Dodgers. I was at my favorite ballpark, Dodger Stadium.

I told my dad I would purchase tickets for my immediate family for the game, but everybody else who wanted to be there had to buy their own tickets. It might surprise you to know that MLB players do not receive free tickets to a game. Even when Jenn comes to a game, I have to pay for her ticket. More than thirty people were there cheering me on that night in L.A., and I knew my dad had been pulling strings all week acquiring tickets so that everyone who wanted to be there could.

I had only one pitch working during that game, a fastball. Through a combination of adrenaline and good fortune, I struck out eight Dodger hitters in four innings. My one at bat proved to be eventful too. Word had caught on around the league that I was not a threat with a bat in my hand. The Dodgers intentionally walked our second baseman, Kolten Wong, in order to face me—it was a quick at bat—so I had to hustle to the plate. I didn't have time to find my batting gloves. It wasn't a huge deal, since I had not been an offensive force anyway and it's doubtful the gloves would have made a difference. But because I didn't have them, I did not have a secure grip on the bat. I swung at a pitch and missed. I actually swung pretty hard, lost control of the bat, and it flew out of my hands, down the third-base side, and landed in the stands. Thankfully, it didn't strike a fan. In order to make sure it didn't happen again, I went to the dugout, grabbed a rag, and loaded my bat with a substantial amount of pine tar to improve my grip.

"I don't think it's legal for a batter to do that," a buddy of mine pointed out to me after the game. I hadn't thought about that and it's a good thing the umpires didn't notice.

I made appearances in eleven major league games in 2018. Twice I was the losing pitcher in a game, and I did not record a win in my first season. I spent the entire month of September with the Cardinals after the rosters were expanded. Anytime I wasn't in St. Louis, I was trying to stay on the minds of the team's decision makers by pitching well in Memphis.

The 2018 season proved to me what I already knew, and thankfully it showed the Cardinals and the rest of the baseball world something I don't think they expected: that I really was a major league pitcher. God took that and multiplied it in a way that only He could, allowing me to have the memorable debut in Cincinnati, pitch well in my hometown of Los Angeles, and finally enjoy the personal breakthrough of being happily married to Jenn. Despite being pregnant and having to watch over a toddler, Jenn would make most of the trips back and forth from Memphis to St. Louis with Casen, staying with me in a hotel. Being a player's wife and no longer just a girlfriend helped Jenn develop real relationships with the wives of other Cardinals. Slowly, we were starting to grow some roots in St. Louis.

During that off-season, Jenn and I welcomed our daughter, Mila, into the world, which was another incredible gift from God. I felt an instant connection to my daughter, and the peace and security I felt in my life at this time surely trickled down to everyone in our home. There was an ease with Mila that we hadn't felt when Casen was a newborn, probably because of the lack of strife Jenn and I had in our relationship. We were a loving married couple. And yes, I tell her "I love you" often. In that off-season, we moved into a new and more spacious house in Florida that gave the kids room to roam. It kept Jenn near her family, connected to the support system that had blessed us through every stage of our relationship.

It was easy for me to sum up the feeling I had in those months leading up to spring training in 2019: I felt blessed. I could see the reward for being true to God. Amazing things were happening in my life that were not part of *my* plan. I had never asked God for kids, and all of a sudden, I had two. Similarly, the house we now lived in was something I didn't ask for, but here it was. Living in a loving, official marriage with God front and center made all the difference in the relationship between Jenn and me. I felt blessed and grateful that during the tougher times in my life, God had protected me, and I had forced myself to take steps to grow as a Christian. I had taken stock of all aspects of my life and realized a dead end was facing me if I didn't wake up spiritually. God had allowed me to find the strength and wisdom I needed at the most critical point in my life, and He had allowed me to thrive in ways I never thought were possible. I believe it was all because I stayed true to Him and His Word.

After spending six weeks or so getting settled into the new house, the next-most-important moment in my career was looming: spring training of 2019. All I had done the previous season was show I deserved a chance to be in the running for a more permanent big league gig in 2019. The Cardinals were loaded with talent and were going to be good with or without me. I had to showcase the intangibles I had as well.

When spring training began, I immediately felt that the atmosphere was different. I sensed the Cardinals were treating me more like a big leaguer, which gave me the freedom and flexibility to make more decisions on how I did things. In addition, they assigned me starting pitching opportunities as if I were a ten-year veteran. I was scheduled to start only games at home or in West Palm Beach, just fifteen minutes or so from Jupiter. How did I reward the Cardinals for that vote of confidence? By having the worst spring training of my career. Every time I took the mound, I got shelled. It literally was an awful month of pitching. I might piece together an inning or two of competence, but then proceed to have a total meltdown and get blown up. After my first start against the eventual World Series champion Washington Nationals on February 24, 2019, I had an ERA of 40.50. ERA stands for "earned run average." It is the average of earned runs a pitcher gives up over nine innings, and it is determined by dividing the number of earned runs given up by the number of innings pitched, then multiplying that number by nine. Things got a little better in March and I eventually lowered my spring training ERA to 7.36, but that was still twice as high as it should have been.

I had stuck with my own throwing program the previous off-season, but it wasn't designed around anything scientific or data-based. I did what I thought was effective, but there was doubt in my mind about my preparation. I was so unhappy with myself, and I knew there was no way the Cardinals were planning on me being on their Opening Day roster. Each morning I expected to receive the news that I was being sent to the minor league spring training camp.

Opening Day 2019 arrived and it felt more like Ground-hog Day as I started my sixth professional season in the minor leagues. It was disappointing, but there was nobody to blame but myself. Late in April, I caught a break. Cardinals pitcher Michael Wacha was injured and unable to make his scheduled start. The Cards brought me up to pitch in one game on April 23 against the Brewers. I packed light because I knew I'd be going right back down to Memphis. This would be my first chance to erase the doubt I had created in the coaches' minds from my horrible spring training, and I think I convinced them that my March meltdown was a fluke. I pitched five strong innings, striking out seven while allowing just two hits and one run.

"There was like a whole different person than I was in spring training," I told the media after the game. "I'm very happy to come up here and perform." This was one of the most important days of my professional career. If I had pitched as poorly as I had in spring training, my future opportunities would have been limited.

My manager, Mike Shildt, was very complimentary after the game. He told reporters I was a big league pitcher who happened to be pitching in the minors. "The reason we were so comfortable and confident with the call to Ponce was his body of work last year," Shildt said. "We know how he's capable of pitching. I loved his body language. I loved his aggression. And I loved his ability to execute his pitches." That was a huge vote of confidence, and fifteen years from now I might look back at that game as being one of the most important turning points in my career.

I returned to Memphis the next day hoping to build on the momentum. I ended up staying in Triple-A until the Cardinals called me up to start a game in New York against the Mets on June 14. Star pitcher Adam Wainwright was injured, and this would be another spot appearance. I was called up to do a job, then probably go right back down. My arm felt alive that night, but the problem was, I had very little control. It was a day where the ball felt electric coming out of my hand but had a mind of its own; hence I racked up thirty-four pitches in the first inning alone. I restored order in the second inning because my second best pitch, my cutter, started working for me, and I could mix that in strategically with a fastball that was hitting the radar gun in the mid-90s.

The game was tied at 1–1 in the top of the fifth. I was scheduled to hit that inning and had my bat in my hand, ready to go to the plate. But there were two men on the bases and only one out, and Mike Shildt felt that this was a chance for us to break the game open. Jose Martinez pinch-hit for me and blasted a three-run home run, leading us to a 9–5 win. I was still fresh and could have pitched much longer, but Shildt made the calculated and correct decision to remove me, and I told the media that after the game. "One hundred percent I could have gone more, but Shildt made the decision and it was the decision of the game," I said. "Great decision by him. That's why he's the manager."

There was a palpable shift in my career now. I was consistently very good and at times dominant when I was playing for Memphis. And I was now 2 for 2 in taking care of business when the Cardinals needed me in 2019. Jenn and I decided that when the future promotions came, she and both kids would come with me to St. Louis. We were packing our bags again a few days after I returned from New York because I was on tap to start a home game against the Miami Marlins on Wednesday, June 19. It's impossible to know how much to pack when you don't know how long you'll be staying somewhere, so we overpacked on this trip like we always tended to. Better to be safe than sorry. I try to arrive the night before my starts so I can be as rested as possible, and we arrived in St. Louis late on Tuesday, June 18. I booked a room at the hotel I normally stayed in in downtown St. Louis, just blocks from the stadium, and specifically requested two beds in a larger room. What we actually received was a reminder that I was still paying my dues and dealing with the same types of issues any family trying to make things work with limited financial resources had. I opened the door and walked into the smallest hotel room I've ever seen, and that perspective comes from someone who played in low Single-A minor league baseball. I know small hotel rooms! There was one bed, a television, and a small walkway to the bathroom. Four of us would inhabit this small space. We called for a rollaway bed for Casen and a crib for Mila, and somehow sandwiched all of this into the unusually small room. Jenn and I unpacked our bags, got the kids into bed, and finally had time to take a shower, brush our teeth, and grab what we hoped would be a few hours of uninterrupted sleep. Well, there was a major issue with our room, and it was the last thing I wanted to deal with. I called the front desk, and it took over an hour to get repacked, moved, and situated in the new room. It was an inconvenience, no doubt, but moments like that keep you grounded, humble, and extremely patient.

Despite the upheaval eighteen hours earlier, I pitched well against the Marlins. My fastball was in the mid-90s and I used it to strike out six Marlins batters. I didn't give up a run, which was important because the score was tied 1–1 in the eleventh inning when Cardinals star first baseman Paul Goldschmidt blasted a walk-off home run to win the game. It felt good to play a role in such an exciting victory. I felt and looked confident on the mound, and I was building trust with my manager, which he confirmed to the media after the game.

"He was fantastic, in control. He's got pitches he can play at this level, and he's proven that. He's earned more opportunities," Shildt said. Thankfully, I'm not a superstitious baseball pitcher, or I'd be requesting unsanitary hotel rooms and long, sleep-deprived nights more often.

By this point in my career, I had been conditioned for disappointment to follow on the back side of big moments. While my faith provides a shield needed to weather these setbacks, emotions can be a powerful force. This big win I played a role in was one of those moments. I received word that, yet again, I would report back to Memphis the following day. As logical as that move was for the Cardinals to make and as much as I understood it, I couldn't help feeling devastated. It's hard to establish a true connection with teammates when I'm essentially a piece of furniture in the clubhouse. There one week, gone another.

As my teammates showered and ate after the game, I found a vacant back corner of the training room and spent five minutes alone. A blend of tears mixed with disappointment and rejection fell down my cheeks. A part of me wondered if this was who I was to them. The spot starter brought in when a real major league pitcher couldn't go. In case of emergency, break glass, and Daniel Ponce de Leon, the minor league pitcher, steps into the lineup for a day or weekend to weather the storm.

Five minutes alone with God was all I needed to collect and remind myself I was actually one of the luckiest people in the world. If it took a few more strong appearances to earn a permanent place on a roster, then that was fine. Ten days later I was back in the big leagues, and this time I would stay long enough to earn my first win. I joined the Cardinals on June 29 in San Diego, in the midst of a nine-game West Coast road trip leading up to the All-Star break. The win didn't come against the Padres. I pitched five relief innings of a game we lost 12–2. This was simply not our night. I struck out nine batters but gave up four runs in what would be the Cardinals' fifth loss in a row. We came back to win the final game of the series, then flew north to Seattle for a series with the Mariners.

Traveling with a major league team is in a different stratosphere from lower minor league road trips. It's like comparing a handful of soggy trail mix to a Thanksgiving Day feast. The only real challenge is changing time zones and arriving in cities late at night. Everything associated with big league travel is designed for comfort, convenience, and making sure players don't have to worry about anything except the next game. After our final game in San Diego wrapped up and we showered, we loaded a bus that took us from Petco Park to the San Diego airport a few minutes away. Next, we quickly boarded our team plane, which is reconfigured so every seat is comparable to a first-class seat. It's impossible to go hungry on a team flight, with multiple menu options available. Upon arrival in the new city, we're bused to a five-star hotel where keys are waiting for our individual rooms. No roommates. No sleep interruptions from snoring or loud phone calls. And definitely no jarring wake-ups on the floor of a bus.

CHAPTER 11

FAITH REWARDED

The road trip continued in Seattle. While the Emerald City is famous for tech, grunge, coffee, clouds, and rain, when the sky is clear, the retractable roof at T-Mobile Park opens to glorious summer sunshine. There are few more spectacular settings to play baseball, let alone reach a personal milestone. That was the backdrop of our game with the Mariners on July 4, 2019. It was long overdue in my opinion, but on this Fourth of July, I celebrated my first career win. Of course, it happened in atypical fashion. One of our best pitchers, Michael Wacha, started but didn't have his best stuff, and I relieved him in the fourth inning, with one out. My job was to prevent the Mariners from blowing the game open. I'm not known for being a pitcher who gets a lot of outs from ground balls, because my fastball has a tendency to rise. This means batters more typically fly out or strike out against me. The Mariners had just taken a 2–1 lead, and they had a runner on first base. I got us out of that inning and retired the first four batters I faced. An unusual set of circumstances led to my recording eight outs during my time in the game, even though I faced only seven batters, thanks to the two double plays our defense turned for us. So, the stage was now set for me to potentially win the game. If our offense could score a couple of runs while I was still the pitcher of record, and our bullpen could hold the lead through the ninth, I would be awarded my first victory. That's exactly what happened. Tommy Edman drove in two runs for us in the seventh inning, Carlos Martinez recorded the last two outs of the game, and I was officially in the win column.

Baseball tradition is a powerful force that can't be denied, and winning for the first time in the big leagues meant I would receive what I call a postgame "condiment shower" to commemorate the occasion. Our manager, Mike Shildt, had been ejected early on, so our bench coach, Oliver Marmol, managed the rest of the game. It was his first win, too, and he would face the same fate. The honored player and coach, in this case me and Oliver, each strips to their sliding shorts, jumps into a laundry basket, rolls into the shower, and after a few words from team leader Adam Wainwright, is ready for the fun to begin. Every other player then proceeds to drench, douse, spray, and pour any and all kinds of condiments or cold beverages on the "honorees" that they can find in the clubhouse kitchen. I knew what was going to happen, so I stripped as I ran down the dugout steps into the clubhouse, happy to be humiliated in any way the veterans wanted. I had residue of ketchup, mustard, mayo, beer, and soda on me when they were done. I'm not positive, but I think Yadier Molina hit me with some hot sauce, too, because my eyes were watering. I loved every minute of it.

The road trip wrapped up in San Francisco right before the All-Star break. After that, Jenn, Casen, Mila, and I spent two days in L.A., then flew to Memphis and packed up most of our belongings and moved them to a new apartment we had rented in St. Louis. I had appeared in six games for the Cardinals so far, and we took the calculated risk and prayed that we would be needed in St. Louis most, or even all, of the second half of the season. We left one bed for me to crash on and nothing else if I had to return to Memphis. Our furniture may have been in St. Louis, but in no way did I feel secure. Even now, there's an always-present thought in the back of my mind that I'm pitching for my career every day. I take nothing for granted because I know how quickly things can change.

On July 12, the first game back from the All-Star Game, my phone rang. When I saw the name on the phone screen, I had one of those moments when it feels like your heart stops beating. A feeling of dread set in. It was pitching coach Mike Maddux. My mind went to a dark place, thinking I was being sent down to Memphis.

"Hey, Mike," I answered.

"Hi, Ponce. I wanted to let you know Waino [Adam Wainwright] can't go today. You're starting," he said.

I checked the time as my pulse returned. It was noon. The game was scheduled for seven. It would be my first start in months, but if that's the role they needed me for, I was going to be the best spot starter in baseball. This game against Arizona had a familiar theme. I pitched well, giving up just three hits and one run in almost seven full innings, but I didn't get the decision. We ended up losing 4–2, but I could take solace in the fact that what I was doing was being noticed. I wasn't racking up a lot of wins, but I was showing almost every time I took the mound I belonged. Mike Shildt told the press, "He was fantastic again tonight," after the game. As long as he was noticing what I was doing, then that was all that mattered.

Anyone who has played baseball will tell you it's a fickle sport. The mental aspects are as challenging and important as the ability to hit or throw a 95 mph fastball. After pitching so well up until this point in the season, I fell into a rut after the Arizona game that had the potential to spiral out of control and jeopardize my career. The stability and consistency I'd shown turned into wildness and unpredictability. I made two starts against the Pittsburgh Pirates, one versus Houston, and the next start I made after that was against Sacramento in the Pacific Coast League. Back to Memphis. That should give you an idea of how those three games went. My body felt crooked, like my hips and shoulders weren't aligned, during this three-game stretch. I just felt off, like I wasn't myself, and that led to three bad outings. I wasn't secure enough to have three bad outings. I remember sitting in the dugout just feeling empty after that Saturday afternoon game against Houston. I felt that I had let everybody down. I had just cracked the rotation and made three starts in a row, and I just didn't get it done. I was worried I'd be sent down after each start against the Pirates and was almost sure I would go to Memphis after the Astros debacle. I gave up five runs, walked four batters, and didn't record a single strikeout. I wanted to figure out what I was doing wrong because I didn't know where the ball was going when it left my hand. I waited for the clubhouse to clear out after the Astros game. I was feeling lonely and extremely dejected as I wrapped my leg to cover the bruise in the spot where José Altuve had drilled me with a liner. I was going to the film room with the intent of figuring out what was wrong with my body. I would stay there until my eyes bled if I had to.

It turned out that wouldn't be necessary. In another illustration of God perpetually having my back, protecting me Himself and literally sending angels to protect me when I need them, a minor miracle occurred in that empty and deserted clubhouse. Our bench coach, Oliver Marmol, who is also a Christian and a man I respect greatly, appeared out of nowhere and entered the room. Besides our faith he and I had something else in common that will forever bind us; we recorded our first win together in Seattle.

"Hang in there, Ponce," he said. "The team is completely behind you and knows what you can do. Keep your head up and keep working. You're going to be a big part of what we're doing."

That spontaneous pep talk and those words of faith he spoke breathed life into me. It was another moment I thanked God for and teared up. I was planning on spending hours watching tape, agonizing and beating myself up as I desperately tried to find some fundamental flaw in my delivery, but Marmol calmed me down and told me to go home and rest. At that point, I put those three bad performances behind me. I let it go and went home to be a husband and a dad.

I did get optioned back to Memphis, but partly because of Marmol's encouraging words, I arrived with the correct mental attitude. I spent all of August in Triple-A, and I transformed back to the pitcher I was most of the season with the Cardinals. That first game against Sacramento, I set the tone early and had the mind-set to dominate. I pitched seven innings, struck out eleven, and gave up only two hits. I was efficient, in control, and overpowering. It was the opposite of my most recent appearances on the mound in the big leagues. I was named the Pacific Coast League Pitcher of the Month for August, and when the Cardinals expanded their roster and called me back up on September 1, my fourth major league call-up of 2019, I came back to St. Louis to a first-place team, ready to help the club with its playoff drive.

As soon as I arrived in St. Louis, I was on the mound, starting on September 1 in a game we lost to the Reds. Six days later, I threw an inning of relief in a blowout win against Pittsburgh. Then I sat in the bullpen for seventeen days. Watching, waiting, and wondering when I would get in another game. On September 24, we were in Phoenix. The game was in extra innings. It was still tied in the thirteenth inning when I looked around the bullpen and said to myself, "I'm the only one left. They have to put me in." I hadn't pitched in over two and a half weeks. I knew I would be rusty, so I entered the game deciding to attack the lineup with one single pitch. It would be Daniel Ponce de Leon's fastball versus the Arizona Diamondbacks. I literally threw nothing but fastballs as hard as I could. I got through three innings without giving up a run. Arizona won the game in the nineteenth, but I had done my job and kept us alive as the game dragged on.

The Cardinals played very well in the second half of 2019 and we entered the playoffs, champions of the National League Central. Major League Baseball teams were allowed to carry forty players on their roster for the month of September. The season is long and grueling, and this gives up-and-coming players opportunities they normally wouldn't receive. It also allows good teams gearing up for the playoffs, like us, a chance to rest some of their stars. For the playoffs, rosters are reduced back to twenty-five. For someone like me, still on the fringe at this point of my career, I obsessed and wondered if I would be included on that list of twenty-five for the postseason. Had I done enough throughout the season, even with all the ups and downs? My agent and I talked about it, but neither of us had received any sort of indication one way or the other if the Cardinals would want me for the playoffs. Jenn and I started slowly packing up the St. Louis apartment and making our plans for the first few weeks of the off-season. Mike Shildt used almost every available minute to strategize and discuss with his coaches and the Cardinals front office which pitchers would make the cut. I had no clue. I could see the argument going either way. On one hand, I had shown the Cardinals that the organization could count on me in 2019. I proved I was a legitimate major league talent. On the other hand, playoff baseball is different, and I was new to it. It would be easy for them to select a veteran with experience pitching in October. Truthfully, I didn't expect to make it, and I was upset because I felt that it was completely out of my control. I pitched only three times in the month of September. I remember a reporter asking me how I felt and I said, "I'm upset. I didn't really have any opportunities to pitch [in September] so how will they know if they want to use me in the postseason?"

We were scheduled to play the Braves in the first game of a National League divisional series on October in Atlanta. The rosters were due on October 2. In the early afternoon of October 1, I was driving back from Chipotle with lunch I had picked up for Jenn, Casen, and myself. I was less than a mile from home when my phone rang. I looked down to screen it. It was a call I knew I should answer, though, as the caller

ID indicated it was Mike Shildt. My career was at a defining moment, and the lump that developed in my throat confirmed it. My long-term future could be determined by what I would hear in the next few seconds. There were two possible messages he would have for me: either I had made the playoff roster or I could head home for the winter. "Here we go," I thought.

I answered the call, expecting to be informed of one of the most important decisions made about my career. I did not receive clarity, though. "I think you've made the team," he said. "We have to have a few more conversations about it, but you'll have confirmation tomorrow."

I hung up the phone completely baffled. It seemed odd that he would tell me something that wasn't yet definitive. He said he thought I'd made the team. That was good. But I was also thinking, "Did the team really believe I could be trusted with the pressure of the postseason?" I had barely pitched the past month. I got back to our apartment and updated Jenn the best I could. We spent the next few minutes sitting on pins and needles while eating beans and rice.

I couldn't allow myself to get too excited or be disappointed, because nothing was official. As I reflect now, it's a real-life metaphor for my life and career. I am resigned to the fact that nothing is easy or typical when it comes to my career. I've learned and expected that. I had asked God to use me in the way He saw fit, and ultimately my steps were predetermined by Him anyway. So I was at peace those final hours because of that. I didn't think Mike would have called me if I wasn't in his plans. The one main factor working in my favor to convince Mike to take a chance on me was that I was a hybrid-style pitcher. I could eat innings if a game was out of hand. I could pitch out of the bullpen in any situation, and make an emergency start if there was an unexpected injury. I was versatile, and my calm nature might give Mike the security of knowing I wouldn't get rattled in pressure situations. Hopefully. I still needed to know for sure, so the next day I went to the ballpark and just asked if I was on the roster. The answer was yes. There was an article in the *St. Louis Post-Dispatch* about the playoff roster, and the reporter referred to my addition as "the lesser of two evils," as the decision apparently came down to picking me over a veteran. Ouch.

Whatever, I had made it. I was part of the chosen twenty-five. The lights were about to get much brighter, and the intensity would be palpable, but we had the type of team that didn't change its approach. We were ready for the playoffs to start. I was excited to play any role asked of me.

The series started and I found myself completely locked in and hanging on every pitch as I watched from the bullpen.

Playoff baseball was totally different and I could literally feel the intensity. The series was tied 2–2, and it came down to a final game in Atlanta. I had yet to make an appearance, but I was more than ready if needed. Whoever won game five would advance to the National League Championship Series to face Washington. We ended all suspense right out of the gate, scoring ten runs in the first inning of game five. There was no doubt we would win the game and the series. Because of the blowout, I expected to pitch at some point, but I never got off the bench. Honestly, I had no problem with it. It was a little odd celebrating with my teammates because, frankly, I hadn't done anything in the series to contribute, but we won, and we were moving on. I was one step from being in the World Series.

Between games, I was basically playing a lot of catch, so I started experimenting with a couple of my pitches. I changed the grip on my cutter and my curveball. I had some extra time, so I was just screwing around, trying different things. I thought those new grips felt good. Good enough that I decided if I got into a game, I would try them out. This was not normal. You would not find many other pitchers who would drastically change two of their pitches in the middle of an intense playoff run and then say, "Hey let's try this now," in a game with the World Series on the line. I never thought twice about it, though.

I believed these new pitches could work, and I was anxious to give them a shot in a game.

The Nationals dominated us. They were peaking on their way to winning the World Series. In game three in Washington, DC, they led 7–1 when I received the call that I was coming in. I soaked up what was an incredible atmosphere. The opportunity was right in front of me now to try these new pitches on the biggest stage of my life. I warned my catcher, Yadier Molina, that he should be ready for something other than gas. "Call a couple more curveballs; I think it might work tonight," I told Yadi as we started the inning. I mixed in these new pitches with my fastball, and I saw results immediately. The added adrenaline was an asset, and I had the Nationals off-balance. I finished with four strikeouts in two innings. It was a solid playoff debut, and I appreciated the opportunity that Mike had given me. But the disappointment of dropping that game and the series—the Nationals won game four the following night and ended our season—made me forget about what I did in my one appearance. As soon as the series ended, I was already thinking about next season and what I had to do to improve for 2020.

Instead of going east to Florida with Jenn and the kids, I wanted to go west by myself for a week. I had hoped to do the same thing the previous year, but I didn't have the money for it. Making the playoff roster meant another revenue stream for me, as I would be awarded a playoff share. Our salaries are paid through the regular season, and during the playoffs, each team is given a set amount of money that is determined by how successful it is in the postseason. That lump sum is then divided among the players and other club personnel. That was another reason making the playoff roster was such a blessing. For those additional two weeks, I made more than my salary for an entire season in the lower minor leagues. That blessing allowed me to take about $6,000 to go to Seattle and spend a week at a data-driven baseball performance center called Driveline Baseball. I had the trip budgeted almost to the penny. I would need funds to cover the training, a flight to Seattle, a rental car, a hotel, and food. I didn't want to spend the time away from my family after an almost nine-month season, but Jenn and I decided this would be one thing that would be worth it. It was an investment in my career that I had to make. The timing was right to do it immediately after the season, while I was still in baseball shape.

Driveline is a next-level training facility with advanced methods and techniques to break down a pitcher's throwing motion, identify what is holding him back, and develop a plan to fix it. Through a combination of unorthodox techniques using weighted balls, max effort, and submaximal throwing, they help pitchers use science and data to improve their form, throwing motion, strength, and confidence. I consider myself a self-made pitcher. That was fine as it got me to this point in my career. But there was definitely another level I was capable of getting to, and my agent and I felt Driveline could help me get there. I had purchased and been using some of their PlyoCare weighted balls, but always under my own training program that was the opposite of scientific. Honestly, I didn't know what I was doing. I knew a week with Driveline would be invaluable, and I would come home with a legitimate throwing plan for the off-season.

I was particularly interested in their biomechanical analysis and having their slo-mo cameras identify any flaws in my delivery. In order to get the readings they needed for their computers, I had to strip down to my sliding shorts and pitch as hard as I could. The fastest I could throw that week while hooked up with wires all over my body was 87 mph, far from the 97 mph I am capable of registering in a game.

My days at Driveline were essentially a crash course in everything I needed technically to become the best version of myself as a pitcher. It was also the final phase of the self-improvement project I began after my head injury. It took some time, and I'm still definitely a work in progress, but I had become a committed husband, a devoted father and family man, and a more edu-cated and informed pitcher. Last but not least, my faith was at a new level.

I was reading Bible passages every day. I was glorifying God for His responsibility for my health and success with each inter-view, sound bite, and response to social media messages. God was at the forefront of everything in my life. Jenn and I were in a great place. Married, with two healthy kids. I also dramatically changed my eating habits by putting more emphasis on nutri-tion and being conscious of everything I took into my body. Everything was coming together.

With my pitching mechanics on point, I could work for three months to take the next big step in my career—become a *full-time* Major League Baseball player. Even though my entire career had been a series of highs and lows and consistently an inconsistent journey, I felt that nothing could stop me now… nothing but perhaps a virus, another obstacle to overcome. Another test of my faith.

I was having the best spring training of my career in 2020. I've never pitched better. And then the season was suspended on March 12 due to COVID-19. Was I disappointed? Sure, but I'll be back…with my faith not fractured.

CHAPTER 12

PLAYING, PRAYING, AND PAYING IT FORWARD

My goal was to finalize this book during the first month of the 2020 baseball season, from our apartment in St. Louis, as an official member of the Cardinals' Major League Baseball roster. There were natural breaks in the schedule that were perfect for it. I could have easily fit in working on this chapter between games of our April series at Busch Stadium against the Dodgers, or even during a road trip to Chicago, Los Angeles, and Denver. But God had another plan. The COVID-19 pandemic stopped the world in its tracks, and I prayed and continue to pray for the safety, strength, and perseverance of family, friends, and fans all over the world. It put baseball on hold, altered the lives of everyone you and I know, and further reinforced for me both the theme of this book and the story of my life—faith.

To understand faith as I know it, the word must be defined. When I need clarity and direction in my life, I turn to the Bible. The definition of "faith" for me is laid out in Hebrews 11:1: "Now faith is confidence in what we hope for and assurance about what we do not see." That verse is so important that I have had it written in the notes folder of my phone for years. Just as faith is my source of strength through dark times, your faith can carry you through the struggles you face. I bet you've needed it more than ever this past year. I had a serious life- and career-threatening brain injury, but your struggles are unique to your life. The faith you have will fuel you through challenges. I recommend reading Hebrews 11 frequently and seeing the examples of faith displayed in that book of the Bible. It's something you can apply to your daily life and, in turn, receive an incredible amount of strength, security, and hope.

Working on this book made me look back at my life and reflect on every trial, tribulation, and experience I have encountered and grown through. I've been knocked down so many times, and faith is the only reason I have been able to get back up. God has used all of these ups and downs I've faced to lay out a plan for my life that I could have never come up with on my own.

I would never have chosen the roundabout path that brought me here. But it's because of that journey that I'm writing this book now. I can't count the number of emails and messages I've received in the past few years that say "If you can fulfill your dream of pitching in the major leagues after what you've been through, I know that I can accomplish anything." Those interactions, with people who are baseball fans and even those who aren't, are the reason I am writing this book.

Writing a book like this is not something I am comfortable with, as I have put every part of me out there in a vulnerable way for people to read about. It took prodding and encouragement from my inner circle, nobody more prominent than Jenn and my agent. But they eventually helped me see that I need to share my story with the world, both to honor the incredible support system that got me through the dark and difficult times, and to honor God. They helped me to understand that my purpose in life is bigger than simply being the best Christian, husband, father, pitcher, and teammate that I can be. It is to use my platform to testify to the powerful work God has done in my life and to share boldly about the power of prayer.

My purpose is to help others understand that God wants to be a part of their lives as well. I want to deliver my message of hope to the broadest possible audience.

No matter what I went through, I always had faith in God and eventually came to learn He had a plan for me even if I couldn't see it. The peace I carried with me to the mound in Cincinnati when I made my Major League Baseball debut in 2018 was a peace I had never experienced in my entire life. Even with the chaos of having that kink in my neck, I was filled with a spirit of calmness that defied logic and was impossible to explain. The peace I received from the prayer I recited that day allowed me to give that performance, which opened every door of opportunity I have now. If I had not pitched that well, there would have been no interest in reading what I had to share in a book. I've seen God work throughout my life. He has rewarded my faith to such a degree that it became the prominent theme of this book. It was an easy choice.

I now understand that I have been given a rare platform as a professional athlete, and I want to use it, to motivate, to encourage and to inspire. That is why I have poured my heart and soul into this book, just like I did during my rehab to pitch again—because I hope to have a positive impact on others in a permanent way.

Low points, disappointments, and failures will happen. Many of mine are on full display in the pages of this book. I hope you can take from my struggles the understanding that they are natural when they occur in your life.

It would be wishful thinking to assume you'll never stumble. But when you have a foundation of faith and know your steps are predetermined, you will recover from the low points quicker, and hopefully even learn from them. One way I do that is by making a conscious effort to stay humble. It's an ideal starting point for everything. The Bible says, "Humble yourself and you will be exalted. Exalt yourself and you will be humbled."

Time will tell where I go from here, but in my heart I know I want to help guide and teach adolescent boys about what it means to be a man in God's eyes. It's a cause that is near and dear to me because millions of children are not exposed to God. My heart goes out to these kids, especially the boys who have to deal with things that were completely foreign to me growing up. Social media is a big problem, destructive in so many ways for our youth. I'm thankful I didn't have to navigate adolescence with social media being as much of a force as it is now. It's so easy for kids to fall into bad habits and not understand what God has designed them to be. I frequently speak to youth and church groups, and I'll continue to do so when given the opportunity.

Do I consider myself a great speaker and enjoy being in front of crowds? Hardly, but my story, my experiences, and the unwavering faith and devotion to God's Word will hopefully help me be an authentic voice. Kids need to be introduced to the Bible and to the teachings of God early on. In many cases, they aren't exposed to either at home and don't go to church with their parents. Many of them will hear about what's in the Bible for the very first time when I speak to them. I try to share with kids that the Word of God provides the wisdom and knowledge they need. It teaches them to act like a man and what's needed to become not only a good person, but a righteous person.

Kids are being swayed toward dangerous influences. The draw and power of that pull is so much stronger in most cases than their exposure to the message that is in the Bible. These kids need a message of hope and love, and any sort of leadership from a positive male figure that they can receive in their formative years is critical.

Being drafted by the Cardinals was a blessing because I was exposed to a team whose name is synonymous with professionalism. They also had several faith-filled Christians on the roster who helped me understand the impact I could have on teammates as I developed my own voice inside the clubhouse. Because the baseball season is so long and we spend almost every day around one another, I need to be transparent with my faith. I have to live the life that I preach, and baseball allows that because we travel, eat, and socialize together. When conversations turn toward subjects I don't want to be part of, I politely leave. I don't shove any messaging down my teammates' throats or anyone else's. Telling someone he needs to read the Bible or act a certain way is counterproductive.

My life is about faith. Your life can be about faith too. Trust God. Trust His Word. It will be there for you when you most need it. How else can we explain how one line drive raised me up instead of knocking me down?

ACKNOWLEDGMENTS

As I have gone through the many ups and downs of my life as recounted in this book, I need to thank God for everything that he has provided to me and my family. My faith has been tested, but, gratefully, my relationship with God has continued to grow stronger every day. I am a proud Christian father because of what He has provided.

The concept and idea of *One Line Drive* was born out of a tragic event in Des Moines, Iowa, but my goal in writing it is to inspire people to never give up, always chase their dreams while trusting that God has a plan for each of us. Therefore, thank you, readers of this book, for reliving the journey and intimate details of my life with me.

Thank you, dad, Ramon Poncedeleon. You have been my mentor and best friend my entire life. You always provide comfort and guidance, and forever have my back. Thank you, Mary, my mom, for taking me to practice as a boy growing up in Southern California and supporting me every step of the way. I couldn't have achieved success in life without you and your dedication and commitment. I don't say it often enough, but I love you both. To my three sisters, Jackie, Bianca, and Julia, I am so glad to have each of you in my life. Separately and collectively, you have been a special part of who I am today and have always helped me stay humble and learn right from wrong.

Thank you, Brian Grieper, my long-time baseball agent, who has helped guide me through my career since the low minor leagues, has been in my corner since the beginning, and who is someone that I consider part of my family. Thank you, Jeff Deutsch, my friend and attorney, who spearheaded the idea of this book and spent more hours than I will ever know protecting my best interests and the integrity of the project while drafting, reviewing, and editing numerous documents and contracts. Thank you, Jan Miller, my literary agent, who believed in my inspiring story from the first time we met and discussed it in Atlanta; and thank you, Tom Zenner, my collaborator, who has put in countless hours interviewing people and then doing an excellent job helping tell my story in a meaningful and faithful way.

Thank you, fans who have supported me during my career, from little league to high school, to my many stops in college, and to the minor and major leagues. Yes, my comeback was first and foremost faith-fueled, but it was fan-fueled as well.

Thank you, John Mozeliak, and the entire St. Louis Cardinals organization, who gave me my chance to live out a kid's dream and become a Major League Baseball player. I am forever grateful for all that the Cardinals have done for me and my family.

Thank you, Scott Ensell, my trainer who made split-second decisions on that fateful day in Des Moines, Iowa, that helped me get back to living a normal life as a person, an athlete, a father, and a husband. Without your incredible medical and emotional judgment, I would not be where I am today.

And to all of my former and current teammates, from little league to the major leagues, who have been on this journey with me, thank you. I love and respect you all!

Most of all, thank you, Jennifer. Without you as my wife, my rock, my number one fan, mother of my children, and partner in life, I would not have been able to accomplish so much or know now that we have still have so much more we can achieve. Together we have overcome obstacles while growing stronger every day. I love you, Jenn. I can't say it enough now! To my children, Casen and Mila, I love you. You are gifts from God. One day you will read this book and know Daddy's story. I hope to continue making you proud.

ABOUT THE AUTHOR

Daniel Ponce de Leon is a Major League Baseball pitcher for the St. Louis Cardinals. His inspiring baseball story includes a long, winding path from high school to the majors, including recovering from a life-threatening skull fracture and brain injury that occurred when hit by one line drive. Daniel was born in La Mirada, California, on January 16, 1992, to Ramon and Mary Poncedeleon. In 2018 he married Jennifer Beatty, whom he met while attending Embry-Riddle University. His surname was originally spelled as one word, Poncedeleon, but he legally changed the spelling to three words, Ponce de Leon, in 2018. A devout Christian and faith-driven family man, Daniel spends the off-season with his wife and two children in New Smyrna Beach, Florida.